THE
HATS
THAT MADE
BRITAIN

THE HATS THAT MADE BRITAIN

A HISTORY OF THE NATION THROUGH ITS HEADWEAR

DAVID LONG

The History Press

To J. Roger Baker (1934–93).
He taught me more than he realised, and
would have enjoyed this a lot.

First published 2020

The History Press
97 St George's Place, Cheltenham,
Gloucestershire, GL50 3QB
www.thehistorypress.co.uk

British Library Cataloguing in Publication Data.
A catalogue record for this book is available from the British
Library.

ISBN 978 0 7509 9381 4

Typesetting and origination by The History Press
Printed in Turkey by Imak

CONTENTS

INTRODUCTION

It was a graded society – and hats told you something. The elegant grey topper and the formal black silk set you apart from the bourgeois felt and the plebeian tweed, the official kepi and the schoolboy's coloured cap
– Philip Mason, *The English Gentleman* (1982)

From trilbies and top hats to boaters and bowlers, a hat reveals a lot about a person's character as well as their country, and much of Britain's social history can be traced through the hats and headdresses of politicians and performers, as well as ordinary citizens.

The oldest known hats are the those found on small terracotta figures belonging to the ancient Indus River Civilisation. Examples discovered at archaeological sites such as Mohenjo-daro and Harappa date back between 3,500 and 5,700 years. At that time hats typically provided protection from the weather and occasionally weapons, although they soon came to play an important role in ceremonials before evolving yet again into decorative garments for the fashionable, the rich and the powerful.

By the Middle Ages there were civil and religious laws requiring hats to be worn, and in Victorian Britain they were such an important part of every self-respecting lady or gentleman's wardrobe that a person would no more leave home without a hat than a pair of trousers or a skirt. Poor people wore them too, of course, and for centuries hats were a visible symbol of a person's wealth, class and occupation, as much for the bowler-hatted city gent as for the lowly farmworker in his cloth cap.

Today they are worn far less often, although it is significant that London's oldest shop is a hatter. Many of the best-loved fictional characters are still strongly associated with the hats they wore, from the Artful Dodger and his battered top hat to Chaplin's famous bowler and even Del Boy from *Only Fools and Horses* with his trademark flat cap.

Hats are so much more important than mere theatrical props or fashion items, however. Many continue to play a role in some of the most deeply embedded national customs, both here and abroad. Graduates still tip mortarboards to their tutors, top hats are still required in the Royal Enclosure at Ascot, a coronation would be meaningless without a crown, and where would Haxey be without its famous medieval leather hood?

The old saying may no longer be true that 'if you want to get ahead, get a hat,' and it's hard to imagine a return to a world where literally everyone wore one. But hats still have a lot going in their favour. They don't just keep us warm, dry or shaded, and looking smart. There's something terribly nice about tipping your hat to a friend or an acquaintance – and there's still no finer way to hail a cab.

MUSCOVY HAT

For a place most people in Britain rarely, if ever, visit, the historic City of London has bequeathed to these islands more than its fair share of common phrases and sayings. Several of these – including 'at sixes and sevens', 'on tenterhooks', 'baker's dozen' and 'if the cap fits, wear it' – have their origins within the Square Mile, these particular ones referring to the customs and traditions of the Livery, the City's ancient craft guilds.

Another saying most of us are familiar with and understand is 'I'll keep it under my hat', meaning to keep something secret or hidden. However, few know its precise derivation, or that it refers to a particular and rather singular item of headgear.

The hat in question is that worn by the City's official Sword-bearer, a ceremonial post closely associated with the Lord Mayor of London who is elected each year by the members of the aforementioned Livery companies. It's an ancient appointment, indeed so old that no one knows quite when the first man was appointed, nor indeed who he was.

The City is known to have possessed a ceremonial sword as long ago as 1373. In 1408 a man called John Credy was given a house rent-free in Cripplegate, in recognition of fourteen years' good service as an Esquire to the Lord Mayor when his duties would have included carrying the sword before the mayor at official functions.

In the centuries when exactly this sort of privilege was granted by popes to sovereign heads of state, the right to have a sword carried before the Lord Mayor was a significant concession to the City and a clear demonstration of its wealth and status. The City's wealth derived from its unique position as the chief trading port of the country (which in a sense it still is). Much of its status, however, depended on its relationship with the Crown. For hundreds of years the sovereign had most of the power but rarely enough money. Successive monarchs soon came to realise that in exchange for special rights and privileges the City could be relied upon to provide piles of it, more than enough to fund their palaces, their pageantry and their wars.

The sword was conceived as a tangible symbol of the privileges that flowed from this relationship, and it is significant that one of the five* in the collection at Mansion House was a personal gift to the City from Elizabeth I. Her Majesty's gift marked the opening of the first Royal Exchange, a vital centre for trade and commerce.

The prize of carrying it was duly given to 'a man well bred … who knows how in all places, in that which unto such service pertains, to support the honour of his lord and the City.' As such, it has always included various responsibilities connected to the running of Mansion House, but it is otherwise expressly ceremonial. Although the sword blade looks real enough, responsibility for protecting the Lord Mayor's person remained with the Sergeant-at-Arms. (It still does today: his immense gold mace was originally a club-like implement, a weapon designed to keep the mob at bay while the Lord Mayor processed through the streets.)

While the heavy mace is a formidable piece of equipment, it is the Sword-bearer who cuts the more imposing figure. Although both officials wear similar black robes and lace collars, the Sword-bearer has the added advantage of a tall and magnificent hat which looks like beaver but is actually made of sable.

This is London's famous Muscovy hat, a name which references the City's historic Baltic trade. Commerce between Britain and the Russian empire was once a source of considerable prestige for London merchants and also of great profit. Much of the profit came from the fur trade, at the apex of which sat the ferocious and ferociously expensive sable, a northern species of marten.

---

* Actually six if one includes the Travelling State Sword, a finely etched replica created in the early 1960s when it was recognised that the Sword of State had become too valuable to be allowed to leave the Square Mile.

King Henry I possessed a sable wreath valued at £100, an eye-watering sum of money in the twelfth century, and in 1520 the Holy Roman Emperor Charles V presented Henry VIII with £400 worth of sable at their much anticipated meeting on the Field of the Cloth of Gold. The king was reportedly so taken with this princely and unstinting gift that on returning to England he declared that henceforth only peers above the rank of viscount would be permitted to wear anything similar.

Evidently the Tudor statute must have expired somewhere between then and now, and merely the fact that the Sword-bearer's uniform includes a sable hat gives a good indication of his status.* This particular hat isn't merely decorative, however, and it is one of its more unusual features that takes us back to the saying quoted above.

One of the many set pieces of pageantry or ritual performed during the Lord Mayor's year is the Silent Ceremony at which the new incumbent is presented with the symbols of his new authority. Lord Mayors these days serve only one term and the ceremony takes place at Guild Hall** on the Friday before the second Sunday in November. It is witnessed by quite a crowd, including City aldermen and officers, masters of the various Livery companies and hundreds of their fellow liverymen. A few tickets are made available to the public.

The whole thing lasts no more than twenty minutes but it's a moving piece of theatre. The incoming Lord Mayor speaks when he swears an oath of loyalty, and there's a fair bit of foot-shuffling and the muffled clearing of throats, but it is otherwise

---

* Despite an extensive breeding and reintroduction programme in parts of Siberia, these animals are still rare and their pelts extremely costly. Because of this even the so-called sable-hair brushes favoured by watercolour artists are not actually made of sable, but of weasel hair.

** Observant visitors to this, the oldest secular building inside the Square Mile, will notice that above the south door the arms of the City are shown surmounted by a Muscovy hat rather than the usual helm and crest.

conducted in almost total silence. The actual transfer of power from one Lord Mayor to the next occurs at the precise moment that one dons a black tricorne hat (p.43) and the other removes his or hers.

It is then that the assembled officers take turns to present their respective symbols – including the Crystal Sceptre, the Sword and the Mace. Each officer takes three steps forward and bows three times before presenting the symbol. The new Lord Mayor touches each in turn, after which the officer walks backwards, bowing again as the process is reversed.

When it's the Sword-bearer's turn, he removes his famous hat and carefully takes a key from a concealed pocket in the underside. This is the key to a safe containing the seals of the City and Christ's Hospital. The Sword-bearer hands the key to the retiring Lord Mayor, who in turn hands it to the incoming Lord Mayor, who immediately returns it to the Sword-bearer with a request that it be kept safe. The key is then returned to the pocket for another year, and the Sword-bearer puts his hat back on his head.

HAXEY HOOD

North Lincolnshire's annual Haxey Hood Game has been played for several hundred years and could well date back to the Middle Ages, although this has so far proved impossible to verify. The game is thought to relate to a story involving the wife of the 3rd Baron de Mowbray, the overlord of the nearby Isle of Axholme, who is said to have lost her red silk hood to the wind while out riding on Christmas Day in the 1350s.

Thirteen local smallholders or 'boggins' reportedly gave chase and eventually retrieved the hat, which was returned to the lady. Grateful for this act of gallantry, she promptly rewarded each of them with a selion (a narrow strip of land used for growing crops) but insisted that they pay a symbolic or 'quit' rent for these by re-enacting the chase each year.

However, some ascribe the festivities to a pagan rite, suggesting the original hood was the bloody head of a sacrificial bull; others claim to have identified Christian symbols in the proceedings, suggesting the willow wand carried by the Lord of the Hood (see below) represents the twelve Apostles. Whatever the truth, the game takes place each year, on the twelfth day of Christmas.

It begins with a procession towards the part-Norman church of St Nicholas accompanied by ringing of the bells and the singing of traditional songs such as 'Drink Old England Dry' and 'John Barleycorn'. At the head of the procession walks the Fool, soot-faced and dressed in a red shirt, patched trousers and colourful decorated hat. He carries the sway hood, a 2-foot-long leather cylinder, and once the procession has reached its destination he stands on a stone mounting block by the churchyard wall to welcome the crowd and explain the game, chanting:

Oose agin' oose, toon agin' toon
If tha' meets a man, knock 'im doon
But don't 'urt 'im*

---

* 'House against house, town against town, if a man meets a man, knock him down but don't hurt him.' The towns are the two local villages, and the houses their respective pubs.

Apparently this last line was only added a century or so ago after some near-fatalities among the thirteen boggins. These days two of these, the Lord and the Chief Boggin, wear hunting pink and top hats decorated with flowers. The Lord also carries a wand or staff as his badge of office, made of thirteen willows bound with thirteen withy-bands.

The game begins on a piece of rising ground between Haxey and Westwoodside, close to the place where Lady de Mowbray was supposedly riding when she lost her hat. The hood is thrown high into the air and as it comes down a sway (or scrum), which these days can number more than 100 players, does whatever it can to push, pull and shove the hood down off the hill. The object of the game is to get it to one of four local pubs that have taken part over the last 100 years or more.

Once underway the game is raucous, it's very noisy and it looks rough – but there are rules. These forbid players from running with the hood and it mustn't be thrown or kicked. The boggins are responsible for rounding up any stragglers and do their best to prevent damage to village property (not always successfully). The Lord of the Hood acts as referee, policing the rules. Depending on the energy and commitment of the players, many of whom look like very useful members of local football and rugby teams, it can take several hours to manhandle the hood towards one village or the other.

Because of this, the latter stages of the game have frequently been conducted in near-total darkness, which can make it even more hazardous than usual for those still watching. Historically the game was declared to be won only when the licensee of one of the pubs could reach out and touch the hood from his or her front step. Unfortunately three of the four have since closed.

CAP OF MAINTENANCE

Most clearly seen on the arms of the city of York is an item described in Heraldic French as a '*chapeau gules* turned up ermine'. This is a ceremonial cap, made of crimson velvet lined with ermine, which accompanied the grant of a ceremonial sword to the city, probably by Richard II in the late fourteenth century. This was an unusual honour but not unique, although the cap now on display in the Mansion House is a much later version and was presented by George V in 1915.

George V's gift to York was specifically intended to be worn by the city's official sword-bearer and is a copy. The genuine cap of maintenance forms part of the royal regalia. It is kept in London and as a symbol of the sovereign is carried before the monarch at the State Opening of Parliament each year, usually by the Leader of the House of Lords. Significantly, it is only worn by a new male sovereign as he makes his way to and through Westminster Abbey to be crowned.

When it was last used for this purpose, at the Coronation of George VI in 1937, the cap was removed immediately before the anointing ceremony and then replaced by the seventeenth-century St Edward's Crown.* In its place, and much as her great-great-grandmother Victoria had done more than 120 years earlier, Queen Elizabeth II wore the George IV State Diadem for her journey through Westminster. Rather lovelier than the cap it replaces, this incorporates various national symbols – including roses, shamrocks and thistles – as well as 1,333 diamonds totalling 320 carats and 169 pearls, several of which were rented from the makers by George IV. It is usually on display at the Queen's Gallery at Buckingham Palace.

---

* This is a replacement for the original, which was melted down for scrap by Cromwell after the murder of Charles I. It is nevertheless regarded as a holy relic because of its association with Edward the Confessor and is worn only for the actual coronation. Immediately afterwards, the new sovereign puts on the lighter Imperial State Crown (p.207) to leave the Abbey.

The origins of this tradition, and indeed of the cap of maintenance itself, are not well understood. One theory is that caps of this sort were granted by the Pope to both Henry VII and his son Henry VIII as a mark of special privilege. Another suggests a more practical purpose: that a soft cap of this sort may have been worn simply to ensure that the heavy jewelled metal crown was more comfortable and stayed in place.

York is unusual in displaying the cap on its arms, but it is by no means the only city to have been honoured in this way. Bristol, Coventry, Lincoln, Newcastle upon Tyne, Norwich, Worcester, Hereford, Exeter and Hull have also received swords. Their official bearers wear an assortment of different headgear when on duty, the most interesting of which is almost certainly that awarded to Waterford in southern Ireland by Henry VIII.

Now a prized exhibit in the city's Medieval Museum, this early-sixteenth-century hat is made of Italian velvet from Lucca and stiffened using whalebone. It is decorated with gold bullion and has an embroidered Tudor rose on top and daisies around the brim. These are known to have been a favourite of the king's, a reminder of his grandmother, Lady Marguerite Beaufort. Her name comes from the French for daisy, and it was Marguerite's descent from Edward III that provided the Tudors with their slender claim to legitimacy.

The hat is genuine and was awarded to the city in thanks for its loyalty during the Dublin rebellion of 1534. It may well have been created for this specific purpose, but if not, if it was a truly personal gift from the head of the king, it is almost certainly the sole survivor of Henry VIII's extensive wardrobe.

THE LUM

Inverkeithing near Dunfermline, one of Scotland's ancient royal burghs, hosts the Hat and Ribbon Race each August as part of its Lammas celebrations* to mark the beginning of the annual harvest.

The event is thought to have been held in the town since early medieval times, originally for shepherds or 'herd laddies' and farmhands who used to flock to Inverkeithing to hire themselves out for the coming year. The race is run over a road course of just under half a mile up and down Hope Street and the prize is a lum for the winner, the Scottish name for an early kind of felt hat, and colourful ribbons for his girlfriend.

Ahead of the race each year a top hat is paraded around the town accompanied by a marching band and carried to the finishing line on the end of a halberd. It is presented to the winner by the Provost of Fife, and these days anyone local can enter, providing they are 15 or over.

---

* From the Anglo-Saxon *half-mas* or 'loaf mass'.

CANTERBURY CAP

No longer seen quite as often as used to be the case, the Canterbury cap or 'catercap' is an ecclesiastical garment and takes the form of a soft square with sharp corners. Designed to be practical and foldable, it forms a traditional part of an Anglican priest's garb and is usually worn with a cassock or soutane during processions and for outdoor services such as funerals or Palm Sunday.

Early examples of the type can be seen clearly in several Holbein works (including a celebrated painting of Sir Thomas More*) and in the National Gallery's famous 1545 portrait of Thomas Cranmer, the earliest known work by Gerlach Flicke. As Archbishop of Canterbury, Cranmer was one of the leaders of the English Reformation under Henry VIII, Edward VI and, briefly, Bloody Mary. However, it wasn't until the seventeenth century that headgear similar to his own began to be more widely adopted by ordinary parish priests. Its name almost certainly reflects the earlier popularity among heads of the Anglican Communion.

The caps are traditionally made either of velvet, for bishops and doctors of divinity, or of wool for the lowly parish clergy. Unlike vestments, which change colour with the seasons, Canterbury caps are also usually black although there is a single royal blue one among the more than 500 items of clerical headgear on display in Germany's astonishing Philippi Collection.** This particular one is an English design, made in central London, and was intended to be worn by choristers.

To most modern eyes the cap is easily confused with the Roman Catholic biretta, but viewed from above it has four radiating ridges on the top instead of only three. Although both

* His actual hat has survived and, together with one of his teeth, it was displayed at the St John Paul II National Shrine in Washington, DC in 2016.
** The world's largest collection of clerical, ecclesiastical and religious head coverings is located at Kirkel in Saarland. It is privately owned and can be viewed only by appointment.

hats were and often are still made by exactly the same clerical suppliers, and notwithstanding that both descend from exactly the same medieval prototype, the differences between them – stylistic and symbolic – are clearly significant to their respective wearers.

The bestselling author of *The Parson's Handbook*, for example, was very keen to remind his readers of the foreignness of the 'positively ugly biretta' which he said, 'offends an immense number of excellent lay folk'. It's possible or even likely that Percy Dearmer was right about this when he first wrote it in the nineteenth century, but it is hard to imagine that much, if any, offence would be taken these days. That said, his influential *Handbook* has so far run to at least a dozen editions and has rarely been out of print. It may be significant that the same ringing assertion is still being made more than 120 years later, both digitally and in book form.

Whether he's right or wrong about this, the caps do appear to be slightly controversial even now. Only eight years ago an Anglican parish priest wrote to the *Church Times* defending his decision to wear one, saying he did so even though his own wife had told him he looked ridiculous in it, and that his local MP had accused him of having 'a strange Tudor sartorial fetish'. Similarly a website which claims to keep 'loyal Anglicans safe from superstition' states quite clearly that the Canterbury cap is nothing less than an affront and that anyone wearing one is doing it only to 'show his disregard for Reformation ideals, Anglican order, and English values'.

Happily, the cap's close relation seems to be more generally accepted. This is the College Cap (or Oxford Soft), and it is a reminder of the once close relationship between the Church, State and academia.

Today the cap is often worn as an alternative to the rigid mortarboard (p.109), especially by female students who for a long time were prevented at some universities from wearing mortarboards. Its yielding, floppy shape has been likened in the past to an apple turnover, although an upside to this is that it can usefully double as a pencil case at institutions where students are required to wear subfusc for examinations (usually meaning a commoner's gown over a sober suit). Oxford University regulations insist that caps be worn during indoor ceremonies – when mortarboards can be carried – but the rules at Cambridge are less stringent.

KIPPAH

The male skullcap or yarmulke* is one of the defining symbols of modern Jewish identity, although it is mentioned nowhere in the Old Testament and religious authorities have been arguing since at least the Middle Ages about precisely when and where it should be worn.

Many of the most observant Jews wear theirs all the time; others put them on only in order to fulfil the requirement for men to cover their heads while at prayer. No one doubts the importance of this last thing, although it can seem strange to Christians that they remove their hats to pray whereas Jews put theirs on.

The idea is certainly ancient. It is recorded in the second Book of Samuel that King David covered his head when he went barefoot and weeping to the Mount of Olives, and since the mid-sixteenth century rabbis have advised men in their congregations to walk no more than four cubits, just over 1.8 metres, with their heads uncovered.

Because of this, most synagogues keep a supply of *kippot* for visiting gentiles and they are sometimes given as souvenirs to non-Jewish guests at family celebrations such as weddings and bar mitzvahs (Jews are assumed to have their own). In form it is somewhat like the *zuchetto* ('little pumpkin'), a simple brimless, domed cap worn by Roman Catholic clergy.

This too dates back to the Middle Ages, although at that time the decision about what to wear was taken out of Jewish hands more or less completely. Instead, for several centuries, they and Muslims living in Europe were required by harsh, restrictive Papal laws to distinguish themselves from Christian subjects through their clothing. Thousands of Jews in many different countries were compelled to wear distinctive peaked hats and sometimes yellow stars of the sort later revived in Nazi Germany.

---

* A Yiddish word which is possibly derived from the Aramaic phrase (ארי אכלמ) meaning 'fear the King'.

Laws of this sort were barely needed in England, because here the entire Jewish community, one which could trace its roots back to Roman times, was expelled by an edict of Edward I (in 1290). They were not readmitted until 1657** but England wasn't the only country to take such drastic steps. Spain followed suit in 1492 – the poet Robert Graves found 'strong historical evidence' that Columbus was secretly Jewish and had set off to find a new homeland for his people – and four years later Jews were banished from Judenburg in Austria. This time the order came from the Holy Roman Emperor Maximilian I, even though the town's very name means 'Jewish borough' and its coat of arms depicts a Jew in a pointed hat.

Unlike the reviled hats and yellow badges, however, the kippah has always been something Jews choose to wear. It is nevertheless no clearer even now whether the choice to keep heads covered is based on הֲכָלָה (i.e. Halakhah, Jewish law) or merely גהנמ (*minhag*, meaning Jewish custom). This longstanding confusion could explain why the style and make-up of *kippot* vary widely, ranging from simple silk and velvet domes to elaborately embroidered or crochet items. All of them are considered acceptable, as is the widespread practice among fedora- and homburg-wearing Jews of putting a kippah on underneath it.

** The king's motivations were largely financial: once the Jews were banished, their possessions and property reverted to the Crown. Oliver Cromwell's reasons for bringing them back were much the same. He was convinced the return of the Jews would bring great financial benefits to England.

FLAT CAP

A garment which has proved as appealing to working-class wearers as it has to lovers of country sports, the wedge-shaped flat cap has a surprisingly long history. It owes much of its success to a 1571 Act of Parliament that was intended to protect sheep-rearing at a time when the wool trade was a critical component of the Tudor economy.*

For nearly three decades anyone over the age of 6 was required to wear a woollen hat on Sundays and religious holidays. The Cappers Act of 1488 already made it illegal for English subjects to wear ones made abroad, on pain of a large fine, the only exceptions to this being 'maids, ladies, gentlewomen, noble personages and every lord, knight and gentleman'. These classes were still free to continue buying fancy foreign items; indeed, the 2nd Earl of Essex, who could never be accused of numbering excessive thrift among his many faults, boasted six beaver hats from Canada, ten of velvet and a further five of taffeta. Other aristocrats sported large hats 'like the battlements of a house' which were decorated 'with a great bunch of feathers of diverse and sundry colours'.

There was nothing new about this sort of class-based discrimination, and it wasn't determined solely by the cost of exotic materials. In the Middle Ages ordinary people had actually been forbidden from dressing above their class, and this new law was enforced by means of a fine of three farthings. This was less than earlier punishments but it was still a meaningful amount for servants and so forth, and equivalent to three-quarters of an old penny or about 0.3p.

The law turned out to be difficult to enforce though, and it was reversed before the end of the century. By then, however, head coverings of various sorts had already become ubiquitous, boosting domestic wool consumption in precisely the way

---

* In 1564–65, cloth accounted for a staggering 81.6 per cent of exports from England. Most of this was wool, as the only other fabrics available at this time were flax, hemp, cotton and (only rarely) silk.

its promoters had intended. These gradually gave way to the modern flat cap, usually of tweed or corduroy, which quickly became a signifier of low status. By the mid-twentieth century they had become firmly associated with the likes of the lazy and feckless 'Andy Capp' character in the *Daily Mirror* and with longstanding stereotypes of The North as a grim, grey place filled with whippet owners, racing pigeons and working men's clubs.

The stereotype ignores the fact that Edward VII, George V and George VI all raced birds; the Queen still does and the Royal Lofts at Sandringham House are among the most successful in the country. It also ignored the decline of the traditional urban working class. In the late 1950s a politician's wife noted that, when her husband gave a pre-election speech to factory workers in the Midlands, 'the audience was full of cloth caps all of whom listened enthusiastically.' But once the tweed original began to give way to beanie hats and baseball caps, often worn back-to-front, flat caps were far more likely to be seen out on sporting estates than in the inner city.

It is also significant that, even here, where once they were worn only by loaders and beaters, the guns all began wearing them too. In 1981 the 6th Duke of Westminster, one of Britain's greatest landowners (and a very fine shot), was pictured wearing one while shooting on his newly acquired grouse moor at Abbeystead in Lancashire.** By then it was the natural accessory for all serious shooters, not just dukes, and it is fast becoming so for anyone on a weekend away with a waxed Barbour jacket and a pair of green Hunter wellies. Only time will tell whether or not this new stereotype will prove to be as enduring as that of the pigeon fancier nursing his pint of Warwicks Milk Maid Stout while talking to his whippet.

** The bag on the opening day of the 1915 season was 2,929 birds from eight guns, a record which has never been surpassed.

PLAGUE DOCTOR'S HAT

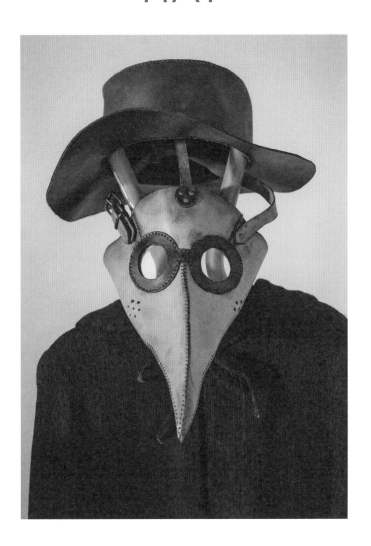

Some of the most chilling images from the Great Plague are of so-called plague doctors dressed in their bizarre, funereal black costumes. Like an early sort of hazmat suit, these comprised long waxed-fabric or leather overcoats, protective leggings, boots and gloves (sometimes smeared with lard). A broad-brimmed black hat signified that the wearer was a physician and was tethered to a shroud with a creepy beak-shaped mask.

Small glass panels covered the eyes and the 'beak', which could be 6 inches long (15cm) and was stuffed with aromatic herbs, hay and spices before being put on. The outlandish ensemble is thought to have been invented about forty years earlier by Charles de l'Orme (1584–1678). He was physician to the Medici family and later to three French kings,* as well as to several members of French society including the writers Guez de Balzac and Nicolas Boileau-Despréaux.

De l'Orme was as highly educated as he was well-connected. He spoke several languages and published a number of learned theses while still a student at the University of Montpelier. Unfortunately, in medical matters his ideas were really no more advanced than anyone else's at that time. He prescribed a deadly poison, anti-mony, to extend the life of Louis XIII (His Majesty was dead by 41) and subscribed fully to the 'miasma' theory of disease.

This posited that diseases were caused (and infections spread) by something called miasma, a deadly vapour present in the air and which was believed to contain suspended particles of decaying organic matter. The theory originated in the Middle Ages and explains why malaria is so named – from the Italian *mala* (bad) and *aria* (air). No one seriously questioned the idea for several centuries and it was only supplanted, finally, by germ theory in the 1800s.

At the time of the Great Plague (1665–66) physicians still firmly held on to the idea that the lethal nature of miasma was characterised by its foul smell. So long as an individual couldn't

---

* Henri IV, Louis XIII and Louis XIV.

smell anything nasty, de l'Orme and his fellow professionals supposed, no harm could come to him. With this in mind the Frenchman recommended a mask 'shaped like a beak, filled with perfume with only two holes, one on each side near the nostrils, but that can suffice to breathe and to carry along with the air one breathes the impression of the drugs enclosed further along in the beak'.

Stuffing the beak with sweet-smelling herbs and spices was meant to prevent any harmful odours, or what were called 'pestilential effluviums', from reaching the plague doctor's mouth and nose. That way he couldn't catch anything – including bubonic plague.

Of course, no amount of lavender, mint and camphor was going to work, and it didn't.** In less than eighteen months, the plague had killed around 100,000 Londoners, or about a quarter of the population. This suggests a far better survival rate than the fourteenth-century Black Death (which killed 200 million worldwide, and up to 60 per cent of all Europeans) but no evidence has ever come to light showing that plague doctors fared any better than ordinary citizens.

Many, in any case, weren't proper doctors or even apothecaries. With panic sweeping up through Europe, city authorities knew they had to do something. Visiting the houses of victims carried enormous personal risks, and the richest, most successful medical practitioners could afford not to hang around. Few did: according to a contemporary estimate by one of its members, four-fifths of the College of Physicians were 'in flight from the capital'. As a result, new recruits were mostly impoverished second-raters or younger men with very limited experience. Doubtless there were others too, chancers and charlatans with no medical training whatsoever.

** De l'Orme wasn't the only one. In London, Dr Nathaniel Hodges kept a nutmeg in his mouth while seeing patients and drank glasses of sack (fortified wine) 'to dissipate any beginning lodgment of the Infection'.

In one sense this probably didn't matter. People naturally hoped to survive the epidemic but probably few expected to, and fewer still knew what it was. The medical profession such as it was certainly had no effective cures to offer, but their distinctive appearance during the epidemic caught the attention of at least one contemporary poet, who recorded it for posterity.

> Their hats and cloaks, of fashion new
> Are made of oilcloth, dark of hue
> Their caps with glasses are designed
> Their bills with antidotes all lined
> Their hats and cloaks, of fashion new
> Are made of oilcloth, dark of hue
> Their caps with glasses are designed
> Their bills with antidotes all lined
> That foulsome air may do no harm
> Nor cause the doctor man alarm
> The staff in hand must serve to show
> Their noble trade where'er they go.

The 'staff in hand' was another signifier that the bearer was a doctor as well as a means of removing patients' clothing to carry out an examination without touching anyone. This was all done free of charge (as they were paid by the authorities) and as public officials plague doctors sometimes witnessed the last-minute wills of the dying.

Occasionally the less scrupulous among them offered expensive quack remedies to anyone who could afford to pay for these. None worked and some were actually dangerous, so that often the plague doctors' sole useful contribution was to keep tallies of the dead, which could be used to map the progress of the disease as it migrated from one part of the city to the next.

De l'Orme, by the way, nearly made it to 100 and for a long time his costume became associated with performers in the *commedia dell'arte* (specifically a character called the 'Medico della Pesta'). Masks like his also make regular appearances at the Venice Carnival, which has helped them to become the most enduring and most recognisable component of this extraordinary garb.

That they have done so is ironic, because modern medical opinion is that literally everything else the plague doctors wore would have been more effective at warding off diseases. We now know that bubonic plague was spread not by bad smells but by fleas carried by the rats that flourished in the 'most beastly durtie streets' of London and other big cities. We also know that floor-length leather coats, hoods, hats and gloves would have made a surprisingly effective barrier against flea bites, and that being oiled or waxed (or even larded) meant that they could also have been wiped clean between appointments.

TRICORNE

The tricorne* or cocked hat arrived in France from Spain as a consequence of the War of Devolution. The war had seen Louis XIV's army successfully overrun the Spanish Netherlands, only to then be compelled to return them to their former Habsburg rulers following the Treaty of Aix-la-Chapelle in 1668.

Before the war, Spanish soldiers had worn hats with wide, floppy brims. These got in the way whenever a musket was held at the shoulder, so troops began to fold (or 'cock') the brims which were then bound into a triangular shape. The result was more functional, and the broad, brimmed gutters channelled rain away from the face. It was also more popular and was quickly copied by the victorious French troops, who took the style back with them to France. Similar hats were soon being worn by the Sun King and his courtiers and the fashion quickly spread not just to England and its colonies but right across Europe.

Here as in France, cocked hats first became standard wear for aristocrats attending the court of Charles II and then a routine part of ordinary civilian dress, as well as being taken up by the army and the Royal Navy. The best ones were made of beaver-fur felt, often richly decorated, but much cheaper ones were manufactured using plain, dyed wool. This meant that essentially the same style of hat appealed to both the nobility and the general population, an unusual versatility that goes a long way to explaining its success and eventual near-ubiquity.

Gentlemen and nobles attending the English court at this time were required to wear a long coat and knee breeches, a 'petticoat' (meaning a waistcoat), a cravat, a wig and a hat. The cocked hat looked good with the style of wig then in vogue, and expensive embellishments of gold, silver and exotic

---

* Sometimes 'tricorn', although neither of these terms was used until the 1850s, by which time the three-cornered hat had largely fallen out of fashion.

feathers gave its aristocratic wearers another opportunity to display their taste and refinement, and hence their social status.

Decorating the folded brim enabled a nobleman to match his hat to the colour and style of the rest of his apparel, but this could be expensive and when a hat belonging to the diarist Samuel Pepys blew into a puddle the replacement cost was a shocking £4 10s. To help avoid the expense, one ingenious hatter offered customers the chance to borrow up to three hats per year. These were 'dyed, drest and cocked in the genteelest manner' for a charge of 15s (75p).

Robert Crofts, the King's Featherman or *Plumarius Regis*, made an especially good living sourcing ostrich feathers for his master, and in an age when all classes wore hats almost all the time it was perhaps inevitable that hat-makers in London would eventually demand their own trade guild. The Worshipful Company of Feltmakers finally received its Royal Charter in 1667, many members having previously been under the control of the Haberdashers.

Theirs could be good business. The cocked hats bought by the Nottinghamshire baronet Sir Thomas Parkyns (1663–1741) were reckoned to cost 22s apiece, or about the same as a skilled artisan might hope to make in a month. Sir Thomas was a wrestling enthusiast and not a bad one either, although his monument in the local church shows him lying prostrate on the floor having lost a bout to Father Time. Decidedly eccentric, he employed two full-time wrestlers at Bunny Hall and offered a lace-trimmed hat to anyone who could beat one of them, and 3s (15p) if they lost.

As well as being handsome, the tricorne's relatively small size and low crown meant it could be tucked politely under one arm in social situations at which seventeenth-century etiquette demanded that a gentleman remove his hat.* Also, because the folded brim was usually simply pinned, laced or buttoned into place, a person of the lower classes travelling on foot had the option of loosening the sides, which could then be dropped down to give some protection from the weather.

In England they were usually worn with one point facing forward, fine examples of which can be seen in several works by Hogarth and in Thomas Gainsborough's early portrait of an Essex landowner and his wife. *Mr and Mrs Andrews* was painted around 1750, by which time soldiers (and pirates) were turning theirs through a few degrees to prevent them snagging on their musket barrels when they stood to attention.

Military versions often sported a cockade or rosette of knotted ribbon, often to indicate the wearer's rank or regimental affiliation, and the expression 'to mount the cockade' came to mean signing up to serve. Under Charles I cockades had generally been red, and then white when Charles II acceded to the throne. William III favoured orange ones during his reign (he was Prince of Orange as well as King of England) but George I insisted on black although naval offices were allowed oval cockades instead of circular ones.

Civilians too experimented with a variety of different styles and colourful brocades over time. Brims could be plain or dressed with gold or silver galloons or braid, and although most tricornes were made of black felt, grey and tan both became popular. Cheaper versions were usually left unlined but the most stylish men-about-town often favoured vibrant silk linings. When the 4th Earl Ferrers was hanged for murder in 1760 his hat and the hangman's noose were placed inside his coffin.

---

* George Fox determined that Quakers would not remove their hats in the presence of royalty; accordingly William Penn kept his on at court only for Charles II to remove his. When asked why he had done this the monarch replied, 'Friend Penn, it is the custom here that only one person wears his hat in the King's presence.'

Tricornes were occasionally known as Egham, Staines and Windsor hats, from the position of the three towns relative to each other on a map, and their popularity lasted for well over 100 years. George Washington wore one when America gained its independence in 1776, so too did all of his immediate successors. The fourth of these, James Munroe (who occupied the White House from 1817 to 1825), even acquired the nickname 'the Last Cocked Hat' because of his preference for anachronisms such as curly, powdered wigs, tricornes and knee-breeches.**

Here the tricorne began declining in popularity towards the end of the eighteenth century, although George III still carried one when he and Queen Charlotte sat for the artist Henry Edridge in 1802–03. Later still, the 8th Earl of Bridgewater left one to each of his servants in his will, along with instructions to keep the household running for a further two months as if he were still alive, although by this time (1829) the tricorne was seriously out of fashion, even for servants. In civilian life it gave way to the top hat, and in the military arena to the bicorne and later still to heavier, taller hats like the shako (p.93). The latter was thought, albeit without much justification, to offer slightly better protection to the head of a soldier in the field.

Today three-cornered hats still form part of the uniforms of many of those occupying traditional offices – Ripon's Sergeant at Mace and the city's ceremonial Hornblower to name just two – as well as any number of town criers and the odd Toby jug. For hundreds of years the aforementioned horn on its elaborate baldric has been blown four times every night from the obelisk in the Yorkshire town's main square (and three more times outside the mayor's house), but outside Ripon the most recognisable tricornes are probably those worn by London's very traditionally attired Chelsea Pensioners.

** Munroe died in 1831 and is the last US president never to have been photographed.

Construction of Sir Christopher Wren's Royal Hospital began in 1682 as a gift to the army from a grateful Charles II. Today it is home to around 300 retired soldiers, men and women* who between them have given literally thousands of years of dedicated service. Known as In-Pensioners, they surrender their pensions on arrival. In exchange they are given private cabins (small but en suite) and privileges which include their own restaurant, club and bar (with free beer on the late king's birthday), allotments for those who wish to take up gardening, and even a bowling green.

As residents of the Royal Hospital or In-Pensioners, the men and women also receive new uniforms which include two frock coats, one dark blue and one scarlet. The blue coat is worn within the hospital grounds and while visiting the local area, usually with a row of medal ribbons and a shako. On ceremonial occasions, however, or if the pensioner travels further afield, he or she dons white gloves and the trademark scarlet coat and a tricorne hat made, like the Lord Mayor's, by the venerable Patey company in Southwark.

The shako was introduced to the hospital relatively recently, in 1843 when breeches were replaced by trousers. But many other ancient traditions have been maintained at Chelsea including the practice of saluting with the hand furthest away from the saluting officer. This is done by way of respecting the old medieval custom whereby knights raised their visors so others could identify them. This was always done using whichever hand least obscured the face.

---

* Women were admitted for the first time in March 2009. The first two arrivals were Dorothy Hughes (85) and Winifred Phillips (82).

BICORNE

A clear descendent of the tricorne, the bicorne first appeared in the 1790s. It was originally worn athwart or sideways-on, most famously by Napoleon Bonaparte* and Admiral Lord Nelson, but within a few years it turned through 90 degrees into the style favoured by another of the Corsican's nemeses, the Duke of Wellington.

In fact, senior officers all wore this sort of cocked hat at the time, army and navy staff officers as well as their commanders-in-chief. Politicians also did, including Henry 'Orator' Hunt MP (1773–1835) who wore an unusual white one as a sign of his political radicalism. Thereafter bicornes remained standard issue in many of the world's navies until the Second World War, albeit only as part of senior ranks' full-dress uniform. Lord Louis Mountbatten was pictured wearing one to good effect on board the Royal Yacht *Victoria and Albert* in the presence of George VI, the young Princess Elizabeth and the Duke of Kent, and the Royal Navy only abandoned them in 1956.

More recently, the mayor of Woodbridge in Suffolk has been filmed being arrested in his robes and bicorne (in 2019), but in Britain the most famous example is undoubtedly the one worn by Nelson on his column. Perched more than 50 metres above Trafalgar Square, this country's great naval hero gazes with his one good eye towards Westminster Abbey, looking past the ships of his fleet which are represented on the iron lamp stands that line Whitehall.

Carved three times larger than life by E.H. Baily, Nelson's likeness is unusual in that most statues of the great and the good in the capital are hatless.** It was given a cheerful makeover in 2012 as part of an installation called HATWALK. To celebrate

---

* Napoleon owned at least 120 hats, only nineteen of which are thought to have survived. Most are in museums but in 2014 one of his bicornes was sold for \$2.4 million to a South Korean collector.

** Including the one of Earl Haig in Whitehall. In this case the absence of a hat caused a flurry of indignant correspondence in *The Times* in 1937 because he is wearing full dress uniform.

the Games of the XXX Olympiad, twenty of the capital's most famous statues – from William Shakespeare to Winston Spencer Churchill – were decorated by leading British milliners. Baily's Nelson was given a new Union flag bicorne, complete with a golden Olympic torch.

Some Londoners found the idea gimmicky and *The Daily Telegraph* amusingly likened it to 'the sort of jape that Bertie Wooster might have committed after a night at the Drones'. But Nelson's was undoubtedly one of the more successful ones – the patriotically coloured replacement made a welcome change from the pigeon-splattered original – perhaps because it had been specially created for the occasion by Lock & Co., the company responsible for all of Nelson's best-known hats.

A brilliant strategist but, like Mountbatten, somewhat vain and egocentric, Nelson took great care to dress well. Fearful of being killed in battle while improperly turned out, in November 1800 he walked into the St James's Street shop determined to buy one of its fashionable two-cornered hats. This was the first of several visits. Clearly pleased with his purchase of 'a cocked hat and cockade 7 1/8th full', he returned a couple of months later to order another which he wore at the Battle of Copenhagen.

Nelson's success against the Danish fleet accelerated his promotion from baron to viscount, but it was to be several years before the admiral returned to James Lock once more. His next visit was in August 1805 to discuss the design of another new bicorne, one with a very specific modification.

In 1794, while besieging a fortress at Calvi in Corsica, Nelson had been blinded in one eye. Vain as ever, he disliked eye patches but sought to conceal his injury by having a permanent shield attached to his hats. To meet this unusual request, staff at the shop conceived a semi-circular felt flap or cover which could be stitched to the underside of the hat's brim. More than two centuries later, the company still has the original hand-drawn design for this in its fascinating archives.

Nelson collected the finished article a few weeks later, and made his final visit in September 1805 to settle his account before sailing for Spain and one of the most celebrated battles in naval history. He took the black beaver hat with him to Trafalgar (with its 'cockade and green shade, 7 full') but would never return to England or St James's.

On 21 October, Nelson lost his life to a musket ball fired by an anonymous French marksman from the mizzen-top of the seventy-four-gun *Redoubtable*.* His body was brought back in a barrel of rum or brandy and, after several days of national mourning, he was buried in St Paul's Cathedral. It turned out that most of the alcohol had been filched by sailors as soon as the barrel was sealed, but somehow, incredibly, the hat survived and can still be seen today on the admiral's wax effigy in Westminster Abbey.

Members of the French *gendarmerie* were still wearing bicornes in the original side-to-side fashion until the very early 1900s, and Italy's *carabinieri* still do this today. In Britain this showiest of hats is largely restricted to those appointed to positions of high honour and dignity by the sovereign. Examples include Her Majesty's Constable of the Tower, an important ceremonial position dating back almost to the Norman conquest. Appointees are usually retiring field marshals (meaning generals nowadays) although in the past the senior office within the Tower of London has been held by senior politicians and even churchmen.

The constable's uniform includes a bicorne with a magnificent plume of swan feathers and is similar to those worn by holders of another ancient office, the Master of the Horse, and

---

* The Frenchman's name has never been verified, but Nelson's death was avenged moments later by either Midshipman Pollard or Midshipman Collingwood on the *Victory*. Conflicting reports mean it is impossible to know which of them fired the fatal shot.

by all governors of Britain's overseas territories and the officer commanding the Royal Hospital, Chelsea.

For sheer dash its only possible rival is the ostrich-plumed Tudor bonnet worn by the Garter Knights for most contemporary bicornes are nowhere near as splendid, and holders of less exalted offices typically have to content themselves with hats which are much less decorative.

The one worn by the Bargemaster of the Company of Watermen and Lightermen, for example, is simple plain black felt, and while the role of Hereditary Lord High Admiral of the Wash sounds decidedly grand (and qualifies for a modest amount of gold trim) his family long ago surrendered the perks and privileges that made this wonderfully arcane post worth having.** The House of Lords still keeps a small supply of plain black ones. These are for use when new peers are introduced (the only tricorne belonged to the Lord Chancellor) although this tradition has been gradually dropping away since the abolition of the hereditaries.

** The antiquated admiralty has passed from one member of the le Strange family to the next since the thirteenth century. Its survival is charming but they are no longer permitted to claim ownership of the foreshore from the high-tide mark to as far out as the incumbent can throw a spear.

TAM O'SHANTER

Hat-making was well established in Scotland in the sixteenth century – by the end of it, bonnet makers in Edinburgh, Aberdeen, Perth, Stirling and Glasgow were all organised into artisan guilds – so this particular type of round bonnet was being manufactured by the Scots long before anyone thought of borrowing the name of the disreputable protagonist in the famous narrative poem penned by Robert Burns in 1790.*

Originally guild members were largely involved in the manufacture of so-called blue bonnets. This was a broad, circular cap favoured by Lowland farmers and labourers, so it was very much a working hat for the masses. Each was knitted by hand in a single piece using thick, rough wool. After being dyed using woad, a plant-based pigment, the hats were felted to provide better wet-weather protection.

The bonnet's form expressly mimicked the more expensive velvet hats worn at this time by lairds and noblemen but its simpler, peasant origins meant it appealed to numerous political and religious radical groups. These included the seventeenth-century Covenanters who decorated theirs with red ribbons and cockades to distinguish themselves from their royalist opponents.

The bonnets only spread to the Highlands very gradually and various different forms evolved. These included the Balmoral or Kilmarnock cap and the Feather bonnet, both of which went on to become popular with Scottish infantry regiments, and the aforementioned Tam.

This too was hand-knitted in one piece and then felted after being stretched on a wooden disc to produce the distinctive flat shape. To begin with, tams were also dyed using woad (and sometimes indigo derived from the plant *Indigofera*

---

* This is one of two sartorial connections. The record-breaking tea-clipper *Cutty Sark* also takes its name from the poem, specifically from the nickname given to the witch Nannie Dee because of her cutty (short) sark (shift).

tinctoria) but they could be distinguished from their humbler forebears by the addition of a tourie, a kind of small woollen pom-pom fitted to the centre of the crown. Tweed and tartan versions only arrived much later, the latter after the repeal of the 1746 Dress Act which for nearly forty years had made any kind of Highland dress illegal north of the border.

Eventually the Royal Family led the revival of traditional Scottish dress (beginning with William IV, as a way of connecting with his Stuart ancestry) but by the start of the nineteenth century the descendants of the blue bonnet were in danger of dying out. Even the tammy was displaced, no one valuing its association with the country's national poet. A mass of more fashionable, factory-made alternatives arrived, leaving local artisans struggling for business.

In 1825, in an entry in his pioneering *Etymological Dictionary of the Scottish Language*, the lexicographer and philologist John Jamieson described tams as being 'formerly worn by the more antiquated peasantry'. Elsewhere reference was made to 'a degenerate form … worn pretty generally by ploughmen, carters and boys of the humbler ranks.'

Salvation only arrived with the rise of German militarism under Kaiser Wilhelm II. In 1915 a military version was introduced for Scottish regiments fighting on the Western Front. Actually closer to a Balmoral but officially designated 'Hat, Tam O'Shanter' or just 'TOS', this was a khaki, machine-made cap initially knitted but later constructed in pieces using woven serge. It quickly became standard issue for Scottish troops as part of their working or field dress uniforms, for use when uncomfortable steel helmets could be safely removed. It is still worn by members of the Royal Regiment of Scotland and by a small number of Australian and Canadian regiments with ancient Scottish connections. Different colour touries or hackles (clipped feather plumes) are commonly used to mark out the different units.

GLENGARRY

In the 1850s this became standard issue for several British Army regiments north of the border, but its origins are older. It takes its name from the Glengarry Fencibles, a militia raised in 1794 as a way of employing Catholic Highlanders who had fallen on desperately hard times after the Clearances, and is often worn as an alternative to the tam o'shanter.

The cap takes the form of a traditional Scots garment made of thick-milled woollen material, usually sporting a tourie on top, which is red, royal blue or black depending on the regiment. Most have a rosette-shaped cockade on the left-hand side and often a red and white diced border, possibly in commemoration of the 93rd Sutherland Highlanders' stand at the Battle of Balaclava – the famous 'Thin Red Line'.

In this form the glengarry came to be worn by pipers in every Scottish regiment except the Black Watch, initially steeply angled to one side but later worn level on the head. Colours have always varied: most were blue; only the Cameronians (Scottish Rifles) wore rifle green until that regiment was disbanded in 1968.

For a while it was displaced by the Universal Pattern Field Service Cap, a side cap similar to the ones worn by Scott, John, Virgil, Gordon and Alan Tracy on *Thunderbirds*, but the glengarry has been worn by members of the Royal Regiment of Scotland since its inception in 2006 . It is also issued to male staff at the Palace of Holyroodhouse, the Queen's Official Scottish residence, and worn by musicians in many civilian pipe bands.

TOP HAT

It's unlikely now that anyone will ever be able to prove the veracity of the colourful yarn about the Strand clothier John Hetherington, who was fined £500 in 1797 after his new top hat caused a riot, and in truth the early history of this particular type of headdress is unusually confused.

A century after the alleged riot, the *Hatters' Gazette* was still describing how Hetherington had appeared:

> ... on the public highway, wearing upon his head a tall structure having a shiny lustre and calculated to frighten timid people ... Several women fainted at the unusual sight, while children screamed, dogs yelped and a younger son of Cordwainer Thomas, returning from a chandler's shop, was thrown down by the crowd which collected and had his right arm broken.

It seems likely that Hetherington had made the first fine, lustrous silk shag that year, known as hatters plush, but frankly £500 is an absurd amount of money for the time. The salary of the Governor of the Bank of England was less than that for the year, and it is hard to imagine anyone, or any dog, becoming so overwrought about a hat.

In fact, no one can be entirely certain quite when top hats began to appear, who created the first one or where he got the idea for something which made such a clear and radical departure from the conventional (and long-lived) tricornes and bicornes.

Every source suggests a different story, but a reasonably strong case can be made for George Dunnage and his partner Thomas Larkin, who claimed to have created a tall hat in 1793. The pair obtained a patent for it the following year and documents exist showing that, not long after this, their company in

London supplied the 3rd Earl of Egremont* with a 'waterproof silk hat', possibly for his coachman.

However, a similar claim is also made for an unnamed Parisian hatter, and a top hat of sorts is clearly shown in Carle Vernet's 1796 painting of two French gentlemen. This was possibly an evolution of the *capotain* worn by Puritans and others, and it became known as the *incroyable* ('the incredible'), although no one in France seems to have been quite as shocked by the idea as one is asked to believe we were in London.

Whatever the truth, tall hats of a similar type quickly gained wide acceptability on both sides of the Channel. They also acquired a variety of different nicknames, including stovepipe, plug-hat, chimneypot and *tzylinder* (in Yiddish) for no one called them top hats before the 1850s.

Before this date, the self-styled 'leader of fashion' Beau Brummel and his 'Dandiacal Body' nearly all wore them. Often theirs were extravagantly coloured, and six are depicted in the wonderful 1820 print, *Well Known Bond Street Loungers*. As crowns grew taller and brims narrowed – the kind but notoriously eccentric 5th Duke of Portland favoured a version nearly two feet tall – top hats began cascading down through the classes, and did this so successfully that it is now difficult to imagine Isambard Kingdom Brunel without his one on, or indeed Eliza Doolittle's dustman dad.**

By the middle of the century the top hat had ceased to be a fashion item and had become routine and entirely respectable. Most if not all were by this time black and straight-sided, like staid Prince Albert's, and for the next seventy years or more this became the default choice for the professional and upper

---

* J.M.W. Turner's great patron inherited the title and spacious estates aged 12 and went on to father at least forty illegitimate children. His only legitimate child, a girl named Elizabeth, died in infancy.

** In *My Fair Lady* (1964). Not everyone wore the best silk, of course. Prices at L. Moses & Sons, the precursor to Moss Bros., ranged from 2*s* 6*d* to 5*s* 6*d* for a 'very fine one'.

classes, especially in town. The prince's connection with the style is important. By choosing to wear one he broadcast a signal to Victorian England, that top hats were now respectable and required. Also the now-traditional black felt band, correctly known as a 'mourning band', was introduced only on his death.

Charles Dickins hated what he called the 'hermetically sealed, black, stiff chimneypot' with a passion and Edward VIII as Prince of Wales wore his at a jaunty angle, which even Eton schoolboys knew not to do, but the factories making them could be enormous. Christy's in Bermondsey employed more than 200 people – making it one of the world's largest hat factories – and the style endured for decades.

In 1908 a Tory MP resigned from his new club in embarrassment after turning up for his first visit in a panama only to discover the other members were all wearing top hats. Around the same time, one aristocrat claimed that by not wearing one in London he saved himself £300 a year in tips. In fact, it was only in the 1920s that sales of top hats began to be threatened by the appearance of softer, more informal hats. The latter were preferred as morning suits started to give way to City pinstripes, although it took until the Second World War for the top hat really to go into serious decline.

Even then it continued to be a normal part of conventional diplomatic dress* and the civilian members of the Japanese delegation to the USS *Missouri* all wore them during Japan's 1945 surrender to General Douglas MacArthur, Supreme Commander for the Allied Powers. They were still being worn in one corner of the City of London until the mid 1980s, where tall hats made stockjobbers easier to identify when share-dealing became frenetic.

---

* In 1943 the Soviet Union, uncomfortable with 'bourgeois society symbols, which are totally alien to the spirit of the Workers' and Peasants' State', issued its own uniform. This had gold-plated buttons, a dagger and a peaked cap and looked unfortunately like the uniform worn by the SS.

But elsewhere top hats rapidly became a rarity. Eton College abandoned them in the 1940s, and at Harrow only monitors or prefects wear top hats, and then only occasionally. The Royal Family wears them more than most, often as a formal alternative to military uniforms at State occasions, as do staff in the Royal Mews. But today they are rarely seen elsewhere except at weddings, funerals and, in particular, race meetings. At both Epsom and Royal Ascot the debate is still ongoing about black versus grey, which is technically known as 'white' and was introduced by James Lock III in the nineteenth century.

Sitting at the pinnacle of a gentleman's formal wardrobe, the top hat is still, undeniably, a plutocratic and wonderfully extravagant hat and it is hard to conceive of a more perfect advertisement for it than John Singer Sargant's celebrated 1902 portrait of Thomas Lister, 4th Baron Ribblesdale. With his top hat, black stock and riding crop, he came to epitomise the image of the Edwardian aristocrat. Edward VII, a man whose entire evening, in the words of one royal biographer, could be spoiled 'if one of his guests wore the wrong tie', nicknamed him 'the Ancestor' because he thought his appearance was so splendid.

The hat's shape and size make it conspicuous but they have nevertheless occasionally endowed it with some practical benefits too, besides giving London's policemen something to stand on in the early days. America's President Lincoln famously kept letters and bills in one he purchased from Washington hat-maker J.Y. Davis (this is now a treasured exhibit at the Smithsonian Institution) and the Duke of Edinburgh is believed to have ordered one fitted with a small radio so he could listen to *Test Match Special* while attending Royal Ascot.**

** In 2019 a royal aide confirmed to the BBC that people place bets on the colour of the Queen's hat at Royal Ascot and that palace staff have orders to lay out decoy hats of different colours to avoid the actual one being identified in advance.

More than 200 years after John Hetherington stepped out to scare the horses on that cold January day (if indeed he did), it's impossible to imagine the top hat making a genuine comeback, but it's also impossible to imagine it ever disappearing. Buyers still flock to Lock's to be measured for one using the company's fiendish-looking *conformateur*, a complex device which was invented in France by Allié-Maillard and is used for accurately gauging the shape of a new customer's head. Lock's was already more than 100 years old in 1953 when the future Emperor of Japan arrived to be measured ahead of the Queen's Coronation, but, much like the top hat itself, it still does the job better than anything else.

FORAGE CAP

An army famously marches on its stomach, and in their pre-mechanised age most nineteenth-century soldiers quickly learned that feeding their horses was as important as feeding as themselves.

When supply lines became stretched or non-existent this meant foraging or even scavenging, and no officer worthy of his rank would have ignored the sensible American Civil War command to 'feed your horses, feed your men, then feed yourself'. These animals typically require 7–10kg of hay per day* and this could pose an enormous logistical problem when an army was on campaign far from home.

Foraging for food could cost a single regiment scores of man-hours every day. Mindful of this the War Office in London introduced a new, more informal item of military undress in 1811. This was designed to be worn around the camp or depot or when troops were engaged in this sort of menial but essential work (also when soldiers were off duty or walking out). The modest regulation cap was of knitted and felted wool, blue-grey in colour with a white band around the base, although many units reportedly stitched their own using pieces of worn-out uniforms and may already have been doing this ahead of the 1811 order.

More comfortable and practical than the shako and other similarly ceremonial headgear, the simplicity of the forage cap's construction also made it easy to put on and to pack away. As recently as 1970, the writer J.B. Priestley recalled the blue dye of his own cap running down his face when, as a young subaltern, he had waited on parade in the rain for Lord Kitchener (who was running late). But it was otherwise a perfectly practical garment, so it was probably inevitable that before long someone in authority would begin messing around with its design to create something completely different.

---

* They also produce around 16kg of manure every day and nearly 10 litres of urine, which can produce problems of another kind.

Within a very few years the forage cap was largely replaced by the circular Kilmarnock Bonnet (named after the town where it was first manufactured) especially north of the border. Stiffer and more decorative cylindrical caps were also introduced around the same time, often sprouting a peak like a *kepi*, a leather chinstrap and even braiding. Usually worn at an angle, these looked much smarter, especially in the right regimental colours, but really they missed the point and simplicity of the caps they replaced.

Some of the new designs were more popular than others, and a few, such as the Brodrick cap, were downright despised. The latter was introduced in 1902 by St John Brodrick during his time as Secretary of State for War. It was made of dark cloth with a tight headband beneath a stiffened crown of a slightly larger diameter.** Such was its unpopularity, possibly due to its similarity to the German *feldmutze* at a time of rising international tensions, that it was withdrawn less than five years later. Only the Royal Marines retained them up to the Great War. Elsewhere in the ranks hundreds of them were cheerfully burned on barrack bonfires so that relatively few examples have survived to go on display in service and regimental museums. Except as a precursor to the peaked cap worn in the Navy and by a majority of modern regiments, it is probably best forgotten.

** In one sense the troops had a lucky escape: Brodrick's name comes from broderer, one who embroiders. He was a liveryman of the ancient Worshipful Company of Broderers but thankfully left the eponymous caps undecorated.

OPERA HAT

In May 1812 a London hatter named Thomas Francis Dollman attempted to register the design of an entirely new hat, although these days its invention is usually credited to a Parisian rival called Antoine Gibus.

Dolman managed to obtain a patent (No. 3561) for what was described simply as 'an elastic round hat'. Only the crown and brim of this, he said, together with a couple of inches of the main body, needed to be 'stiffened in the ordinary manner'. The rest of the hat was left unstiffened and, according to his patent application, it was 'kept in shape by ribs of any suitable material fastened horizontally to the inside of the crown, and by an elastic steel spring from three to four inches long and nearly half an inch wide sewed on each side of the crown in the inside in an upright position'.

This was not the clearest explanation, but by describing a formal hat supported by an internal arrangement of moveable ribs and springs, Dolman is generally assumed to have been the first to conceive the idea of a collapsible top hat. Unfortunately, his patent was only in force for ten years, and he died shortly after it lapsed. It's not known how many of his hats, if any, were ever made.

Sometime between 1837 and 1840, the Englishman's idea was picked up and improved by Gibus, a leading Paris milliner who, together with his brother Gabriel, successfully patented several novel hat designs, many of them mechanical. The brothers had a business in the Place des Victoires and this had such an excellent reputation, in Britain as well as at home, that when another Frenchman, Meriade Anquez, soon afterwards set himself up in London with shops just off Piccadilly Circus and Trafalgar Square he cheekily attempted to pass himself off as one of their sons.*

---

* The fraudster's business seems to have thrived and he and his French partner had a staff of eleven by the time of the 1861 census. Unfortunately, the partner, Louis Ferry, committed suicide a few years later by taking potassium cyanide. The dead man was charged with 'self-murder' but found not guilty after the judge explained to the jury that he had become deranged.

Recognising that top hats were becoming taller and more cumbersome, Antoine Gibus had become convinced that a collapsible version would be more practical and easier to live with. In drawing up a new design for a hat with a hinged frame he provided more details about the mechanics than Dolman had done. The finished article looked more or less identical to a fashionable top hat when it was extended, but when not being worn it could be compressed so that the crown was level with the brim. This meant the hat could be more easily stowed, for example beneath one's seat during a theatre or opera performance. This explains the popular English name for them, although at this time top hats were still worn as often during the working day as in the evenings, hence the description of the Stock Exchange as looking like 'a forest of chimneys'.

The idea caught on immediately, and for a long time in France it was known as a gibus hat and then – once Antoine's brother had introduced the refinement of a spring-loaded mechanism – as *le chapeau claque*, meaning click- or slap-hat, a reference to the sound made by the concealed framework popping open.

Even in Britain hats fitted with similar devices remained so popular for so long that more than eighty years later, when Dorothy L. Sayers published *Whose Body?* (the first of her books to feature Lord Peter Wimsey), the author still felt able to mention the opera hat belonging to the murderer, a respected surgeon and neurologist called Sir Julian Freke, without needing to describe what it was or how it worked.

The fragility of the hats' mechanisms means that genuine nineteenth-century survivors are now rare despite the huge numbers produced. Understandably, they are highly collectible, although the correct provenance can sometimes be hard to establish. Numerous retailers at the time, including naughty M. Anquez, claimed to be selling the genuine article, original hats made by the brothers in Paris, but the reality is that many different manufacturers began producing similar designs of their own, often with slightly different mechanisms.

JOHN KNOX BONNET

A city the size and age of Edinburgh is bound to have its fair share of strange customs. Since 1861 a 64-pound field gun has been fired from the castle at 1 p.m. each day so that the locals can set their watches accurately. On the first day of spring up to a thousand of them climb to the top of Arthur's Seat to wash their faces in the dew in the hope it will bring them lasting beauty. And students at the city's oldest university receive a tap on the head at their graduation from a cap known as the Geneva Bonnet, which is reputed to have been made from the seat of a pair of John Knox's breeches.

This sort of Tudor bonnet is a familiar sight in academe, because ones just like it are traditionally worn by students who have completed their doctoral studies. But this one is stranger than most, not least because Knox, a leading Calvinist minister and theologian during the Reformation, was never a student at the university.* In fact he died in 1572, a full decade before the university's foundation, something which became a source of some embarrassment about twenty years ago when a label was unexpectedly found inside the aforesaid round, black cap. The label was distressingly modern, early-Victorian, and it read *Henry Banks, 22 Duke Street, Edinr 31 July 1849.* This was especially unfortunate as Knox himself explicitly stated in his will that 'none have I defrauded'.

The discovery was made while the cap was being restored in 2000. A split in the fabric had opened up, presumably as a consequence of the approximately 5,000 head-taps the silk and velvet headdress has to complete each year. Further research sponsored by the ceremonial robemakers Ede and Ravenscroft (est. 1689) revealed that Banks had been a merchant tailor in what has since been renamed Dublin Street, and that the cap had been made by one of his six workers using only nineteenth-century materials.

---

* He is believed to have enrolled at the University of St Andrews and may have continued his studies at Glasgow.

The latter fact immediately extinguished any hopes on campus that the label might simply refer to an earlier restoration but, unsurprisingly, the University of Edinburgh authorities decided to stick with their customary tapping. Even if it had been built on shaky foundations, the little ceremony was popular and it had become an important part of the university's heritage. As important as Cambridge University's dogged insistence that its own ceremonies be conducted entirely in Latin, and hardly stranger than Oxford's determination to continue barring any female graduands who show up with bare legs.

Today it's unclear how many if any students at the university still believe Knox's breeches have anything to do with the silk and velvet bonnet, but there are certainly some who think it was once landed on the moon. It is possible they have confused it with the tiny scrap of MacBean tartan which accompanied Alan Bean and the crew of Apollo 12 there in November 1969.** In fact, all that happened to the cap is that an embroidered patch or badge bearing the university's coat of arms was carried on a NASA test flight and then stitched on to it in 2006. This had been taken on board the shuttle *Discovery* by one of the university's alumni, astronaut Piers Sellers, who graduated thirty years earlier. Sellers also managed to smuggle a university flag on to an earlier mission, a handsome souvenir which travelled 4.5 million miles (170 Earth orbits) before going on display at Old College.

** The precious fragment was entrusted to the care of the Scottish Tartans Authority in Crieff, Perthshire on its return.

BEARSKIN

The most famous hat in the British Army has been worn for more than 200 years, yet neither its extraordinary familiarity nor its longevity has been enough to prevent members of the public from getting its name wrong.

The Grenadier Guards was the first regiment to be granted permission to wear bearskins, after the Battle of Waterloo in 1815, but centuries later civilians still routinely refer to it as the busby. The latter is actually a shorter and smaller fur hat, and of central European origin. It has been worn by some British units, including the venerable Royal Horse Artillery, but many feel it lacks the style and elan of a proper bearskin whose full 18inches height once served to intimidate the enemy and still makes even the shortest guardsman look taller, somewhat smarter and more imposing.

Probably for this reason, bearskins can now be found in around a dozen different armies (not all of them in countries of the Commonwealth) but by far the best known are those worn by the Guards Division. After the victory at Waterloo, the Grenadiers' lead was quickly followed by the Coldstream, Scots, Irish and Welsh regiments in the 1830s, and it is the important ceremonial duties carried out by these units which have given the bearskin its high profile.

This ceremonial role largely consists of guarding the sovereign* and it is this that has made the members of the five regiments the most readily identifiable soldiers in the world, rather than the Brigade's outstanding record of gallantry and military derring-do. Even now, though, few visitors to London

---

* The regiments also play a crucial role in the Tower of London's wonderfully evocative Ceremony of the Keys and, following the Gordon Riots of 1780, they were ordered to supply a small piquet or detachment to guard the Bank of England. The troops were granted the privilege of marching with fixed bayonets past Mansion House and, incredibly, the practice was maintained until 1973. By then the introduction of traffic lights was making the soldiers' nightly march from Wellington and Chelsea Barracks something of a trial.

can tell one regiment from another, and it is doubtful that many locals can either. In large part this is due to the troops' delight-fully anachronistic red uniforms, which from a distance all look much the same, although for anyone who cares to take a closer look there are numerous subtle differences enabling an observer to tell one regiment from the next.

The usual way is to count the tunic buttons. These are positioned singly for the Grenadiers, in pairs for men of the Coldstream, in groups of three for the Scots, of four for the Welsh, and five for the Irish. But another way is to study their glossy bearskins, most of which carry a hackle, the name given to the clipped feather plume which is worn on one side or the other. Grenadiers wear a white one on the left side and the Coldstream a red one on the right. The Irish similarly have a blue hackle on the right and the Welsh a green and white one on the left. Only the Scots don't have hackles.

For tourists visiting Britain, the bearskins have become as iconic as a red bus or black cab, but closer to home not everyone approves and not simply because these now largely decorative items are an extraordinarily expensive piece of military kit. That they are expensive is beyond dispute: each one is thought to cost in excess of £800 (no one will reveal the actual figure) and the Ministry of Defence's own figures suggest that at any one time there are around 2,500 in service.

That's a minimum of £2 million of taxpayers' money right there, or it would be were the MoD to replace them all at the same time (which it never does). Clearly the bill reflects the raw material cost as much as the specialised skill it takes to make what the Army still insists on calling caps. This is because their construction consumes the entire pelt of a Canadian black bear per soldier, or of a female Canadian brown bear in the case of individual officers.

The females' thicker brown fur has to be dyed black, but it's not just the cost which protesters object to. Concern over the numbers of *Ursus americanus* and *Ursus arctos* which are shot just to furnish the Army with hats has made for an even bigger bone of contention.

In fact, the Army top brass insists that that fewer than 150 pelts are purchased on its behalf each year, but this hasn't really helped at all. Nor has pointing out that the pelts are sourced from traditional Inuit hunters, a community licenced by the government of Canada to cull tens of thousands of the creatures every year for reasons which are entirely unrelated to military necessity.

In addition, the Army says, each of its caps lasts for decades, which is why barely 5 per cent of them need replacing each year. The same can apparently not be said of artificial fibres, which in any case don't quite measure up. According to at least one retired general, 'In wet weather, synthetic fibre looks terrible [and] anyway, the Canadian bear is not a threatened species so where is the problem?'

In this day and age it's easy enough to dismiss an old soldier as overly conservative and hopelessly out of touch, but at least one MoD spokesman rode to the bearskin's defence after a series of tests was conducted on a potential fake-fur alternative. 'When it rained,' he said simply, 'it was like a bad hair day.' He also warned that these synthetic materials are badly affected by static electricity, which was 'rather embarrassing when the men passed under power pylons'. When sheepskins were dyed to avoid this particular difficulty, the colour reportedly turned out wrong, and the wool became badly distorted in the rain.

Except for those who believe one dead bear is one too many, these lines of defence sound pretty reasonable, but every serving soldier knows there are plenty of precedents for depriving the Army of what it wants, and it's not always done on grounds of cost.

More than twenty years ago animal-rights groups won a signal victory when the big-cat skins traditionally worn by regimental drummers were replaced with artificial ones. More recently at least two designers, Stella McCartney and Vivienne Westwood, have offered to help create fur-free alternatives.

In the longer term, then, it's beginning to look as though this is one battle the Army top brass won't win, and that the genuine bearskin will eventually be consigned to history. When that happens the Inuit will lose one of their oldest, most illustrious and most reliable customers and, while Britain's decision won't mean the culling will stop, a significant tradition will have been lost for good. Also, the opportunity will have been lost for someone to repeat the trick played by the late Major Jeremy Whitaker, who famously hid an alarm clock in a fellow officer's bearskin, which was set to go off during the Changing of the Guard …

HARRINGTON HAT

Fashion is fine when kept in its place, but the eighteenth-century dandy is an easy figure to disparage. Even before George Bryan 'Beau' Brummell ran out of money, before he lost his good looks, before he called George IV fat and had to flee to France where he died seedy, alone, syphilitic and insane, he must have been a hard man to like. Here, after all, was someone who wouldn't lift his hat to a lady because he might be unable to replace it at precisely the right and most fashionable angle, who refused to face anyone seated next to him at dinner for fear of creasing his cravat as he turned around, and who insisted that his own brother stick to the back streets until he had found himself a decent tailor.

Beau Brummell prized his appearance over everything, but despite this he had both friends and admirers, among them 'Apollo' Raikes, 'Poodle' Byng and the similarly self-obsessed Charles Stanhope, Viscount Petersham (1780–1851). A walking caricature of the lisping Regency buck – the lisp an affectation, like almost everything about him – Petersham was so concerned about making the right entrance that he designed and even stitched many of his clothes himself and was rumoured to have worn whalebone stays while still at Eton.

Petersham left the college aged 15 to take up a commission in the Coldstream Guards before joining the 10th Light Dragoons with Brummell, 'the most expensive, the most impertinent, the best dressed and worst moralled regiment' in the whole of the army.* Militarily he achieved little or nothing, but among his proudest creations as a civilian were the Petersham coat and the Harrington hat (he was heir to the Harrington earldom).

The coat was briefly fashionable, but probably only because his friend the Prince Regent ordered seven of them – in seven different colours for the seven days of the week. The hat proved

---

* The officers were nicknamed 'the Shiny 10th' or 'the Chainy 10th' as a reference to the yards of gold braid and criss-crossed gilt metal decoration on their uniforms.

to be no more enduring and a far more successful innovation was the Stanhope gig, a light, two-wheeled town carriage pulled by a single horse, but that was his uncle's idea not his, and really all we know about the viscount's hat is that it will have been brown.

Brummell bought his hats from James Lock but Petersham decided to design his own and for years wore nothing but brown, apparently because of an unrequited love for a widow called Mrs Browne. His vast collection of brown clothes and brown boots (polished using a mixture of his own invention diluted with champagne) were complemented by elaborate cockades which were dyed to match.

Petersham also had his carriages painted brown, insisted that only brown horses could pull them, and made his coachman wear a distinctive brown top hat. Eventually all His Lordship's servants were ordered into similarly mud-coloured livery** and one can only imagine his disappointment when Capability Brown turned down an invitation to landscape the park around the family's gloomy ancestral home in Derbyshire.

The viscount made a similar fetish of drinking tea (which was brown) and took snuff (also brown) at every possible opportunity. The snuff he kept in an assortment of 365 snuff boxes, one for each day of the year, and he was once heard describing a light-blue Sévres porcelain example as 'a nice summer box, but it would not do for winter wear'. His collection of tea, similarly, was stashed in bespoke caddies all round his drawing room – 'congou, pekoe, souchong, bohea, gunpowder, Russian, and many others, all the best of their kind'. Eventually there were so many of them that a visitor

---

** Stanhope wasn't the only one to do this. The 5th Earl of Lonsdale made his indoor servants wear yellow, and those on his estates were required to repaint their tools and wheelbarrows the same colour. Charmingly, all AA breakdown vans are sprayed bright yellow today because in 1905 the earl, an enthusiastic early motorist, accepted an invitation to become the organisation's founding president.

to Elvaston Castle described the effect as being more that of a shop than a nobleman's home.

Petersham affected a small pointed beard in a bid to look like Henry IV, the seventeenth-century French king, and famously claimed never to go out before 6 p.m. That said, it's hard to see how such a boast squared with an army career spanning more than two decades or with his appointment as a Gentleman of the Bedchamber to George III and George IV. It must also mean he was never able to join his sister Anna for afternoon tea, a meal she is widely credited with inventing in the 1840s when she was married to the 7th Duke of Bedford.

Finally, it goes without saying that, like many would-be trendsetters, he was also an appalling snob. After succeeding to the earldom in 1829, he issued regular warnings to Elvaston's army of more than eighty gardeners that they could show the Queen round 'but admit no one else'. Sadly for him, Victoria never took up the invitation and when the earl died his wife left the Gothic Revival castle, never to return. Today Elvaston is owned by the council (and is falling down) and the park surrounding it is open to everyone, free of charge. Charles Stanhope would have hated it.

ATHERSTONE BILLYCOCK

Commercial hat-making began in the Warwickshire town of Atherstone in Tudor times and received a major uplift with the introduction of felt hats in the seventeenth century.

As a cottage industry, felting had already been going on for centuries and a fabric made using unwoven wool is thought to be the world's oldest known textile. The earliest known reference to felting as a distinct craft in England dates back to 1180, although it took until 1604 for James I to grant an all-important Charter of Incorporation in the name of 'Master, Wardens and Commonaltie of the Art or Mysterie of Feltmakers of London'.

The best felt was made from beaver fur using a method which combined heat, moisture and pressure to make the fur fibres mat together into felt. This was slow and labour-intensive until the introduction of a new process called 'carroting' transformed the industry in Britain by allowing cheaper skins to be used.

Carroting involved taking hare or rabbit skins and treating them with a colourless solution of mercuric nitrate before drying them in an oven. The thin fur at the sides often turned orange when this was done, hence the name. After being stretched over a bar, the skin could be sliced off and the loose fur blown into a perforated, cone-shaped receptacle. This was then treated with hot water to consolidate it and passed through wet rollers. These helped to solidify it into felt, after which it could be dyed and blocked into a hat.

The process sounds complex and was inherently risky because it involved the unavoidable release of mercury fumes. This in turn led to an unusually high rate of mercury poisoning in towns like Atherstone where felt hats were manufactured commercially. The dementia this caused is generally assumed to explain the origin of the expression 'mad as a hatter' but sits uncomfortably with the old belief that rubbing beaver-fur oil into a man's head would lead to remark-able improvements in his memory.*

Despite the complexity of the process, the simplest wool-felt hats had always been low-cost products and they could be made quickly in vast numbers to be sold at home and abroad. Atherstone was well placed to do this: an old milestone in the town put it 100 miles from London, 100 from Lincoln and 100 from Liverpool, and from 1769 the town began to enjoy improved transport links via James Brindley's new Coventry Canal.

In fact, modern mapping techniques suggest the aforemen-tioned milestone may have been more interesting than accurate, but at their peak Atherstone's seven large factories employed upwards of 3,000 workers and turned out hats in the hundreds of thousands. Many of these went for export, particularly to the Colonies and especially to the West Indies and America's southern states, where plantation owners and managers needed a source of the cheapest hats possible for their legions of slaves.

With their round crowns and curled brims, the slaves' hats were called billycocks, although the origin of this term is not known. They tended to be very light, just 4 or 5 ounces (140g) which made them economical to export. They were also suitable for wearing in all weathers, while their basic construction meant they could be made by those factory workers who were not yet fully skilled. This was a major advantage over the fitted cap.

Atherstone's more skilled workers, meanwhile, produced many other hats as well, including some for the army fighting Napoleon, but unfortunately the town's heavy reliance on the Atlantic slave trade soon came to spell disaster.

---

* It may also be relevant that one of the England's official Commissioners in Lunacy was R.W.S. Lutwidge, the uncle of *Alice in Wonderland* author Lewis Carroll. The tea-party Hatter is rumoured to have been based on a staff member at Lock & Co., where Carroll was a customer.

Up and down the country campaigners had been trying for decades to abolish the inhuman trade and when, finally, they succeeded, Atherstone's vast and lucrative market dried up within a few years. Naturally, this left a significant dent in the town's economy. Factories closed, workers were laid off, and parish records (in particular the Vestry Minutes for Poor Relief for the 1830s, the decade when slavery was finally abolished) paint a very clear picture of social and economic deprivation.

Atherstone struggled on and its people continued to make felt hats, albeit on a much reduced scale. The town never really recovered from the abolition, although somehow, after more than a century and a half of factory closures and company consolidations, the very last one – Wilson & Stafford's Britannia Works – managed to avoid closing its doors for the final time until the 1990s.

SHAKO

With a name as foreign as it sounds, the shako developed from the Magyar *csákó suveg*. This was a peaked cap worn by eighteenth-century Hungarian hussars, although it is not clear how or why the sartorial habits of these central European light cavalrymen should have spread so far and wide throughout the regiments of Europe and the Americas.

The first British shako was the type worn by the Duke of Wellington's infantry throughout the Peninsular War (1807–14). It was probably copied from the *barretina* worn by the Portuguese marines and made of lacquered linen. The Iron Duke's troops called them bang-ups, because they were 'bang up to date', but the shako's golden period in the British Army really only began after Napoleon had been packed off to St Helena.

Needless to say, and like virtually all military headgear of the period, it offered fighting troops little in the way of protection against a well-aimed sabre let alone gunfire or shrapnel. Despite being relatively heavy, the shako also failed to give marching soldiers much shelter from bad weather. Fitted with a japanned leather peak, most were made of cloth or thick beaver felt over a leather carcass. This meant they became waterlogged (and even heavier) during a downpour. Efforts were made to counter this particular problem by issuing each soldier with a waterproof cover. This was commonly made of oilskin,* but it was clear from the start that an uncomfortable hat that in effect needed a second hat to protect it really didn't make much sense.

The several decades of relative peace that followed Waterloo go some way towards explaining why such a seemingly impractical garment continued to be issued. The fact that the shako looked smart, and certainly it did, made it perfect for peacetime ceremonial duties. For those in charge, this may have been reason enough for it to have become the standard military

---

* Early oilskin was also heavy and cumbersome, being essentially sailcloth with a top layer of tar.

headdress of most regiments in nearly all of Europe's armies – and for it to stay in service for such an extended period.

In Britain it took until the 1870s for the shako to finally give way to cork and pith helmets (p.97), although these had first appeared during the Anglo-Sikh Wars at least thirty years earlier. Because of this it remained standard issue for many regiments in France, Russia, Belgium, Germany and Austro-Hungary until at least 1914. By this time the Highland Light Infantry and Scottish Rifles were alone in still wearing them at home (and then only on parade) and, although the War Office briefly considered reintroducing them to other units, this plan was hastily abandoned at the outbreak of the Great War.

In happier times, however, when more emphasis could be placed on pageantry and display than actual fighting, the British shako acquired many attractive embellishments and adornments. Becoming more and more showy, examples began to appear with a proliferation of gilt plates and other insignia on the front as well as pompoms, plumes, ball-tufts, metallic lace and metal chin-scales, and elegantly-draped gold cords and chains.

Those worn by officers were especially decorative, which isn't especially surprising, except that the original idea was for similar kit to be issued to all ranks. This was to avoid the problem borne by the previous generation of officers who could be identified from a distance by their bicorne hats. Regrettably this made it easier for an enemy sharpshooter to spot one and pick him off.

Shakos also grew larger and taller over time. A huge hat could make a soldier standing to attention look more impressive (and intimidating) but it conferred no real benefits out on the battlefield. Although never quite reaching the dimensions of a guardsman's bearskin, by the 1820s a so-called Regency shako could be more than 8 inches tall and 11 inches across the crown. Splaying out at the top like a bell, they could be given even greater prominence by plumes as much as a foot high.

More with the other ranks in mind, perhaps, there were subsequently a few attempts to produce something a bit more practical. In 1843 the Albert shako appeared, reputedly at the suggestion of the busily inventive Prince Consort who had a prototype version constructed by Lock & Company.

This had a second, smaller peak at the back to protect the neck from the sun and a very slightly tapered crown. It also featured a revolutionary new side-ventilation system, because normal shakos could be stuffy and Albert reasonably supposed that a hot soldier made a poor soldier. It was still heavy, however, and neither comfortable nor popular. When the War Office turned it down, the editor of *Punch* couldn't resist responding with a rhyme:

> Come away to the Palace and look at the show
> Of elegant garments by Albert and Co.
> And look at the beautiful Infantry hat
> Did aught ever bear a resemblance to that?
> With its side ventilation, intended 'tis said
> To keep all the soldiers quite cool in the head.

Unfortunately, these later designs also failed to offer much in the way of protection from ordnance and London's National Army Museum has a Russian 3.5oz ball on display which is believed to have put a hole straight through the shako of a half-colonel in the Connaught Rangers. Accordingly, in a little over ten years, yet another replacement was proposed. This was called the Albert Pattern Helmet, a fine example of which can be seen in the background of James Tissot's celebrated 1870 swagger portrait of Frederick Burnaby, a pioneering balloonist and a captain in the Royal Horse Guards ('the Blues').*

---

* This has been on display at the National Portrait Gallery since its acquisition in 1933. The painting also includes an example of a regimental forage cap (p.67) on the sofa next to Burnage.

PITH HELMET

White cloth-covered pith or cork helmets were first issued to British troops during the Anglo-Sikh Wars (1845–49), after which their use spread to Egypt, Burma and South Africa as a consequence of further imperial adventures. Mostly these were fairly crudely made devices, which many soldiers began to colour using tea or mud to provide them with a degree of camouflage.

Although officially designated the 'Colonial pattern' helmet, these early hard-shell, high-crowned sola topee (or topi) were not a creation of the Empire. Similar hats known as *salacots* were already being worn by the French and Spanish armies in what were then called Indochina and the Captaincy General of the Philippines. Like the British model, these were made of shola pith, a milky-white spongey substance extracted from a species of swamp bean called *Aeschynomene aspera*. This mostly grows in India and Malaysia and is sometimes called Indian cork. The substance dries to produce a material that has been likened to expanded polystyrene.

Every year in parts of West Bengal thousands of blocks of this are carved by armies of Hindu craftsmen known as *malakar* into wedding garlands, headdresses and religious figures. Because the plant's fibres are exceptionally light, the pith could also be used to manufacture sun hats. This was done by layering the pith into a mould, rather like a child making a bowl using papier mâché, and then gluing it to form a rounded shell. Once hardened and dry, the shell could be removed from the mould and swathed in protective, close-fitting cotton.

The result was lightweight, relatively comfortable and impressively resistant to high humidity. These were all important considerations in the tropics, but unfortunately the military hats' broad brims could make them a little cumbersome. They were also highly conspicuous on the battlefield, even after a khaki version was introduced during the Anglo-Zulu War of 1879, and offered only negligible protection against rifle fire. That said, Sir Robert Sandeman of the Indian Political Service survived after being attacked during an assault on Pathan tribesmen in 1880. He was the Governor General's agent in Baluchistan during the Second Afghan War (1878–80) and his helmet, complete with a bullet hole in its centre, is in the National Army Museum's collection.

Latterly pith helmets have come to be seen as a powerful symbol of the Empire, even of white supremacy, especially in those countries where they were worn by white officers commanding locally recruited indigenous troops or by British colonial administrators, political officers and other high-ranking civilians. This goes some way to explaining the offence caused when America's First Lady wore one to Kenya in 2018, although this regrettable association with the Raj completely ignores the fact that similar helmets were standard issue for many foreign armies as well,* including several belonging to Britain's enemies.

The journalist and explorer Henry Morton Stanley** took a sola topee with him to Africa when he went looking for Livingstone, and for him the hat's appeal was much the same as it must have been in the Indian subcontinent.

A high, stiff crown kept the hat clear of the wearer's hair (or pate) and together with ventilation holes this prevented an uncomfortable and potentially unhealthy build-up of perspiration in hot climates. At the same time, the wide, sloping brim was perfect for keeping monsoon rains away from the face and neck as well protecting the wearer from the heat of the sun. Best of all, the whole thing could be dunked into cold water before

---

* They still are. The US Marine Corps introduced them in the early 1900s and still doles them out at several bases, including its vast facility at Parris Island in South Carolina.

** Sadly, in his declining years, the great adventurer was bullied by his wife and mother-in-law into becoming a Member of Parliament. Stanley wasn't much good at this and later admitted he was simply too old to exchange his 'open-air habits for the asphyxiating atmosphere of the House of Commons'.

it was put on. Once saturated, a good helmet would stay far cooler for far longer as the liquid slowly evaporated in the heat.

Over the course of a century several different styles evolved, both military and civilian. In Britain the original Colonial pattern was replaced by the Wolseley pattern, named after Field Marshal Lord Wolseley KP, GCB, OM, GCMG (etc.) although the late-Victorian Army Chief of Staff had little or nothing to do with the design. Its attractively swept brim was said to offer improved sun protection and it remained part of the Army's regulation dress until the 1940s.

This impressive length of service suggests the Wolseley was something of a success, as indeed does the introduction of the Home Service pattern helmet shortly afterwards. This was really little more than a grey or dark-blue copy, for use in non-tropical areas, and to modern eyes it looks so much like a modern police helmet that the two must be related.

Curiously, British forces were never issued with green pith helmets, even for jungle warfare, although the North Vietnamese Army wore these during the Vietnam War (1955–75). Theirs were more bowl-shaped than the British version, and had lower profiles that were more akin to the so-called Bombay Bowler favoured by Winston Churchill during the North African Campaign. As the name suggests, these were made in India in the 1940s, often using Chinese immigrant labour, but it was never standard military issue, although many British officers bought them (using their own funds) while serving in South East Asia.

WIDE-AWAKE

In the 1850s the pioneering photographer Lady Lucy Bridgeman photographed her brother-in-law, the Hon. Robert Windsor-Clive MP, wearing a broad-brimmed hat with a low crown called a wide-awake.

This enjoyed a brief vogue among artists and other Bohemians in Britain, although it is hard to see a great-grandson of Clive of India fitting this description. A respected local figure, he commanded the Worcester Yeomanry in the 1840s and then won the Shropshire South seat in 1852 (no one stood against him) which he held until his death.*

The expression 'never wear a brown hat in Friesland' is supposed to relate to a traveller who was jostled and pelted with stones after arriving in the district wearing a brown wide-awake. In America the hats were rather more popular, the joke there being that they were made of smooth fabric, i.e. one without a nap, although the name more likely derives from the Wide Awakes, a 400,000-strong paramilitary organisation affiliated to the Republican Party during the 1860 election. They supported Lincoln in his campaign against slavery, and were described by the *New York Times* as, 'young men of character and energy, earnest in their Republican convictions and enthusiastic in prosecuting the canvass on which we have entered'.

In 1872 Charles Darwin's cousin, the inventor and eugenicist Francis Galton, recommended the style in *The Art of Travel, or Shifts and Contrivances Available in Wild Countries*, preferably glazed and with a lining of 'fine Panama grass'. Similarly, in 1908 Robert Baden-Powell singled out the wide-awake for special mention in his landmark *Scouting for Boys*, but the style never really caught on here.

Lord B-P evidently preferred his own khaki Stetson, discovered while he was campaigning in the Second Matabele War (1896–97), and Sir Francis went on to produce an alternative

---

* His grandfather was the charmingly named Other Robert, 5th Earl of Plymouth.

called the Universal Patent Ventilating Hat. This used a valve and a rubber bulb to lift the crown, thereby cooling the wearer's head; others were produced which used a system of levers to achieve the same effect. Galton, who also recommended breaking raw eggs into new walking boots to soften the leather, realised that his invention looked jolly odd but wore one all the time, insisting it was preferable to 'falling in a fit upon the floor'.

INTERNATIONAL CAP

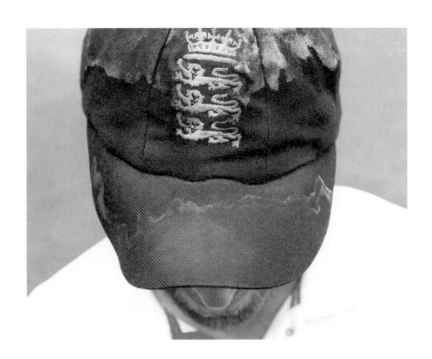

The soft, peaked cricket cap made its first appearance in the eighteenth century and examples can be seen in prints of matches which were played in the late 1700s. In 1845 it received a strong endorsement from Nicholas Wanostrocht, the influential (if eccentric) author of the cricketing handbook *Felix at the Bat,** and similar garments were later adopted by many other sports and numerous schools.

Wanostrocht, an Englishman of Belgian extraction, was a fanatical and talented cricketer, a left-hander who played for Kent for more than twenty years as well as at the MCC, where he became known for his 'cut to the off from his shoulder' and a bowling style that included a particularly deadly slow lob. He invented what was possibly the first ever bowling machines, the Catapulta, which could send a ball towards the batsman 'so fast that it would split your hat in two, or so slow that it would scarcely reach the wicket'. Unfortunately this contraption cost 11 guineas, more than a quarter of the average man's earnings for a year, and it sold very poorly.

Wanostrocht's book was dramatically more successful, as were his patented tubular India rubber gloves and a variety of other pieces of kit designed to protect players against what he called the uncertainty and irregularity of the present system of throwing-bowling. These included 'a cap made of chequered woollen [which] is light and cool to the head, absorbs perspiration and (which is not an insignificant fact) is not likely to be blown off and hit the wicket'.

Wanostrocht's preferred suppliers were Mr Dark at Lord's Cricket Ground and Mr W. Cadlecourt of Townsend Road, Marylebone, but before long the caps were widely available and had become part of every cricketer's travelling ensemble.

---

* The book ran to several editions, the first of which was illustrated by the celebrated Victorian painter and sculptor – 'England's Michelangelo' – George Frederic Watts (1817–1904).

New ones began to be issued to any bowler who took three wickets on the trot, the first going to H.H. Stephenson of the all-England team, who took three for three balls while playing a Hallam side at Sheffield's Hyde Park ground in 1858. It didn't take long for the habit of wearing one to spread to other sports as well, or for the term hat-trick to become more widely used. The caps also became fashionable as ordinary casual wear although this is clearly no longer the case.

Particularly for sportsmen, the fact that the caps could be produced in the multiple colours of the wearer's team, school or club contributed to their appeal, although at the international (professional) level single colour caps are still generally the norm.

The traditional England cap, for example, is very dark blue with the England and Wales Cricket Board (ECB) insignia in white. Australians similarly have what they refer to as the Baggy Green. This sports a colourful coat of arms above the peak which references several of that country's commercial endeavours (wool production, shipping, agriculture and mining) supported by an emu and a kangaroo.

Amidst much debate about who wore the first one and when, the Baggy Green has become much prized as an Australian icon. In 2003 the one worn by the late Sir Donald Bradman during his final 1948 season made nearly a quarter of a million pounds at auction. Shane Warne raised more than double this amount for charity in 2020, by auctioning one following that year's devastating bush fires (£528,514), and according to the *Guardian* newspaper the spin-bowler Bill O'Reilly was so fond of his that he had an image of it tattooed on his backside.

Sadly even this level of enthusiasm hasn't been enough to prevent the traditional style giving way to baseball caps and protective face guards and helmets, the last two a clear response to the continuing 'uncertainty and irregularity of the present system of throwing'. Happily the proper cricket cap has been granted an extraordinary second life, if only by the adoption of the term 'cap' as a shorthand way of describing the relative success of a player's international career.

The practice of awarding new caps to each player before an international match actually began in association football rather than in cricket. A contemporary illustration of the first ever football international – between Scotland and England at Partick in 1872 – shows English players wearing their school caps. The score was a disappointing nil-nil, but it was followed by regular international matches leading to the suggestion that 'all players taking part for England in future international matches be presented with a white silk cap with red rose embroidered on the front'.

The idea came from the Assistant Secretary of the Football Association,* perhaps after he had been offended by the sight of such a variety of different hats on display that day in Partick. Whatever his motivation, it was formally adopted in May 1886 and the practice has since been copied by many different sports around the world, including cricket.

In some sports the cap being presented is a purely metaphorical one, but in others an actual cap is presented to a player once he or she has been selected for an international fixture. Special commemorative caps are also sometimes awarded, for example when more consistently outstanding players reach milestones such as fifty or one hundred appearances for their country, or when the match forms part of a major tournament such as a world cup or regional championship.

In football the current record holders are Egypt's Ahmed Hassan with 184 caps, and Kristine Lilly who has made a staggering 352 appearances for the United States. Cricketer Sachin Tendulkar of India has similarly collected 200 caps in a twenty-four-year Test career and a further 463 for One Day Internationals.

---

* N. Lane Jackson, who also founded the famous amateur side Corinthian F.C. This was the first to field a black player at international level (Andrew Watson, in 1884) and had a centre-forward called Tinsley Lindley who famously played in brogues instead of football boots.

MORTARBOARD

Although wearers of this flat, square scholar's cap typically wear it only once in a lifetime and rarely for more than a couple of hours, its widespread use in Britain and abroad means it has become the most recognisable piece of academic apparel.

The name is clearly derived from the portable wooden platforms used by masons and bricklayers but its origins are impossible to fathom. Possibly it evolved from the Roman Catholic biretta or maybe it developed from one of its precursors, such as the Etruscan *tutulus* or the Roman *pileus*. The earliest European universities were religious foundations after all, institutions intimately connected to the Church where every student was in holy orders.

The hats, almost always black, were certainly being worn in the nineteenth century by academics in Britain and America, but similar garments appeared centuries earlier and may be related. Many Renaissance grandees – senior religious figures as well as military and political ones – sat for portraits wearing tall, cylindrical hats. Looking at Andrea Mantegna's portrait of Ludovico III Gonzaga in Mantua's Palazzo Ducale, or the Uffizi's Urbino diptych by Piero della Francesca, it is easy to imagine how the flared crowns of the sitters' headgear might have developed over time into the stiff squares we see today.

Whatever the mortarboard's origins, it has historically been regarded as male attire, most obviously because universities in Britain did not permit women to sit exams before 1869.* Even when female students were finally allowed to read for degrees, most were obliged to wear Canterbury caps (p.25) instead. It is only in the last couple of decades that they have been able to

---

* In May of that year nine candidates sat the University of London's General Examination for Women, a rigorous test of six subjects ranging from Greek to chemistry. Six of them passed, but it took several more years before women were examined alongside men and awarded degrees. At Cambridge women were not allowed to graduate on equal terms with men until 1948, and remarkably a quota system limiting their numbers was in place until the 1960s.

choose a mortarboard for those rare events at which otherwise ordinary students are required to be properly dressed.

Undergraduates at the University of Oxford need them more than most. Although mortarboards at Oxford are generally carried indoors rather than being worn, male and female students have to attend all formal university ceremonies, including their own examinations, in full academic dress. Even now the rule is rigidly enforced, the only derogation being for members of the clergy and the armed forces, who may choose to wear their own uniforms.

At most other universities students only require a cap, hood and gown for their final degree ceremonies, where it is usual for just the chancellor and other high officials to wear their mortarboards throughout the proceedings. On approaching one of these august figures, graduands need do no more than 'doff' or tip theirs once, a ritual sign of salutation and respect, or nod slightly while touching the front corner.

The mortarboards worn by these high officials can occasionally be quite fancy items. That worn by HRH the Princess Royal, for example, as Chancellor of the University of London, is black velvet with gold-lace trimming and a tassel of gold bullion. Essex University's chancellor is similarly entitled to a bright scarlet mortarboard, edged in gold and with an outrageous broad gold 'fringe' several inches wide.

Depending on the type of skullcap fitted beneath the board, doffing a mortarboard can be harder than it looks. Experienced wearers insist that mortarboards with the older style of rigid skullcap make for a better fit and look smarter. But on the other hand, those with softer, foldable skullcaps are easier to carry and to store. Because of this they have become more common but without a rigid dome it can be a fiddly, two-handed job restoring this sort of hat to the correct position after one has raised it to an academic superior.

Interestingly, the experts at this are probably also the youngest mortarboard wearers of all. These are the ten young boys known collectively as the Children of the Chapel. Together with six 'Gentlemen in Ordinary' they are the choristers who make up the Choir of Her Majesty's Chapel Royal. The oldest continuous musical organisation in the world, this dates back at least to the twelfth century and past members include many of the greatest names in early English music, such as Thomas Tallis, William Byrd and Henry Purcell.

Today the boys, who audition aged 7 or 8 and remain with the choir until their voices break, perform at state and national occasions as well as at private functions for the sovereign and her family. In return they are given a valuable scholarship to City of London School, a scarlet and gold state coat to wear while performing, and a mortarboard. As this distinctive uniform was introduced at the Restoration in 1660, the boys could well be the oldest wearers of mortarboards as well as the youngest.

BOWLER HAT

Its silhouette is as familiar as that of the Beatles crossing Abbey Road and when Charlie Chaplin's trademark bowler hat came up for auction in 2006 the hammer crashed down at nearly £80,000.

The famous hat's first appearance in a movie was back in 1914,* but even then its style was already more than half a century old. The bowler's origins can be traced precisely to 25 August 1849 when a customer called in at James Lock & Co. hoping to obtain some new hats for the keepers on the Earl of Leicester's Holkham Hall estate.

For a long time the identity of the visitor was unclear. The most likely candidate was always the Hon. Edward Coke, the 2nd Earl's younger brother, although for a while it was thought to have been his cousin William. On his visit to the shop that August, Coke explained that the men on the family's north Norfolk estate wore conventional top hats, which looked smart but were easily knocked off and damaged.

He now wished to replace them with something different, something close-fitting and tough. Above all, he said, his brother's keepers needed hats which were strong enough to protect their heads from low-hanging branches while out riding, and from poachers' sticks and clubs when they were patrolling the estate on foot.

Lock quickly had a prototype shell constructed by the company's chief hat-maker, Thomas Bowler, at his factory in Southwark. This had a clean domed shape, with a low crown, rough felt finish and modest brim, and it was shown to the customer in December the same year. Coke approved of the hat's pleasing appearance but he placed it on the ground before

---

* Chaplin assembled his trademark outfit from items he found in the communal dressing room of a Hollywood studio. The baggy trousers belonged to fellow actor Roscoe Conkling 'Fatty' Arbuckle, the size 14 shoes had to be worn on the wrong feet to keep them from slipping off, and the hat came from Arbuckle's father-in-law. Even the moustache had been made for another actor.

jumping on it. Happily, the stiffened brown felt survived this stringent test of its strength and durability and after agreeing a price – 12*s* a head or 60p – an order was placed for more of the same to be despatched to Norfolk.**

The fashion quickly caught on at many other estates. At Eaton Hall in Cheshire, twenty keepers were given bowler hats to wear with their fawn leggings. The head keeper's one had gold braid trimming to mark him out, which was probably also why it was decided that the vast team of eighty estate workers who were roped in as beaters got to keep their wide-brimmed hats of bright scarlet felt.

Today each of the eight keepers employed at Holkham is still presented with a new hat after one year's service, and in St James's Street they continue to call them Cokes (pronounced *cooks*) in honour of the original nineteenth-century buyer. However, further afield, the term 'bowler' has enjoyed far greater prominence especially since the fashion for these hats spread from England's country estates to the capital.

This shift happened surprisingly fast. By the end of the 1800s the bowler had left its rural roots behind and become firmly established as an essential item of weekday wear for anyone who was 'something in the City'. For a long time only official government brokers retained their distinctive silk top hats*** and until well into the 1960s it was still rare to find a photograph of London's Square Mile which didn't include someone sporting a black bowler with a matching, tightly-furled umbrella.

Trains on the Metropolitan Line finally scrapped hat racks and umbrella hooks in 2013, but bowlers and brollies are still the order of the day for Cavalry Sunday in Hyde Park. This is London's annual Combined Cavalry Old Comrades

---

** It's not clear how many of the hats were actually made by Bowler but his factory at 34 Southwark Bridge survived until 1940, when it was destroyed in two consecutive German air raids. The business relocated to Great Marlborough Street W1, and finally closed in 1962.

*** Until 1986 and the 'Big Bang' deregulations.

Association parade and memorial service for the fallen. Serving officers are also expected to wear suits and hats when they are in town on duty, so military personnel still account for many of the 4,000–5,000 Cokes that Lock & Co. sells today. Sadly only one of them has so far seen fit to follow the example of Major Digby Tatham-Warter, DSO, who famously led a charge at Arnhem while wearing his bowler and brandishing tightly-furled black brolly.

This idea of the sophisticated and well-heeled man about town is presumably what the retired officer John Steed hoped to convey in ITV's *The Avengers*. Unfortunately, the bowler's appeal extended to several markedly less savoury characters around this same time. These included Alex and his gang of violent 'droogs' in Anthony Burgess's dystopian *A Clockwork Orange*, *Batman*'s wicked Riddler, and the Korean henchman in *Goldfinger* whose lethal, weaponised version was used to kill Tilly Masterson, decapitate a statue and nearly did for the trilby-wearing James Bond.*

Filmmakers clearly couldn't resist the chance to subvert what had hitherto been an unimpeachable symbol of respectability, and who can blame them? Evelyn Waugh also teased wearers slightly in his second novel, *Vile Bodies* in 1930, with a running gag about imaginary bottle-green ones, but René Magritte's attachment to the style is far harder to explain. The Belgian surrealist artist frequently wore one himself, and between 1926 and 1966 he included bowler hats in his paintings at least fifty times. Yet he always insisted the garment had no meaning: 'It poses no surprise,' he said. 'The man with the bowler is just a middle-class man in his anonymity.'

---

* Oddjob's was actually a heavier Cambridge hat in the film but a standard bowler in Ian Fleming's novel. Two film props were supplied by Lock & Co., and at a sale of 007 memorabilia in 1998 one of them sold for £62,000.

Interestingly, across the Atlantic, bowler hats traditionally carried quite different connotations. What Americans call the Derby was more working class than bourgeois. It wasn't just railway workers and cowboys who wore them but also settlers heading west in their covered wagons, and even outlaws such as Billy the Kid. One can only assume that they too valued a hat which stayed in place when a man was riding, and that this was just as true hitching a ride in a boxcar as it was on horseback.

Stranger still has been the bowler's adoption by the *cholitas* of Bolivia. Women from the indigenous Aymara and Quechua tribes first took to wearing them in the 1920s, possibly because a consignment of hats arrived from Europe which were too small to be worn by British railwaymen working in the country. Together with a colourful pleated skirt worn over layers of petticoats, and an embroidered shawl or *manta* closed by a brooch, these *bombins* now form part of their traditional national costume.

BALACLAVA

Perhaps more familiar these days as a ski mask than as a hat, the original woollen balaclava took its name from the famous battle of 1854. British participants in the Crimean War are known to have worn this type of woollen headgear against the biting cold of the Russian winter, although the name 'balaclava' was not widely used for the garment until the 1880s.

The earliest known name of the settlement closest to the battlefield is Symbolon, when it was an important Greek trading post on the Black Sea shore. By the Middle Ages, control of both the town and its harbour had passed to the powerful Byzantine Empire and the town had been renamed Yamboli. The name was changed to Cembalo when the area was conquered by the Republic of Genoa, and then again to Balyk-Yuva (Turkish for 'Fish's Nest') in 1475, when the Genoese were surrounded and then defeated by well-disciplined troops loyal to the Ottoman Sultan Mehmed II.

It remains a matter of conjecture whether any of these would have been more or less suitable as the name for a hat (or indeed a battle) but it's an interesting question given the number of times this small town has changed hands over the last several centuries. Indeed, the process is still ongoing: at the time of writing the modern town of Balaklava is part of Ukraine, although in 2014 the entire Crimean peninsula was annexed by Russia – for a second time – almost certainly illegally.

The aforementioned battle occurred during the nearly year-long siege of Sevastopol and its naval base. Military supplies sent from Britain were marooned at the ancient port which lies about 8 miles south of the besieged city. Conditions along the road linking Balaclava and Sevastopol made it impossible to move men or materiel forward, and before long British troops were struggling due to a lack of food and with no suitable clothing for the unusually ferocious winter.

Reports of instances of starvation and frostbite soon reached home. Amid rumours that the bitter cold was causing as many casualties as the enemy's bullets, articles began appearing in the press (particularly *The Times*) detailing the privations being suffered as a result of the failure of the British commissariat (a department of HM Treasury) to provide winter clothing. In a response to a loud public outcry over the mishandling of the situation, protective clothing was hastily issued to Lord Raglan's troops.

This included a form of a knitted hood designed to cover a soldier's ears and neck as well the top of his head, which, as every schoolboy knows, can lose more heat than any other part of the body. They were not universally adopted, however, and many of the most famous depictions of the Crimean Campaign show troops in more traditional headgear. These include the bearskins in Robert Gibb's *Saving the Colours, the Guards at Inkerman* and shakos in Thomas Jones Barker's *The Rally, Balaclava.**

For those who did chose to wear them, the new garments looked a bit like a softer, more comfortable version of the mail coifs which knights in the Middle Ages wore beneath their helmets. They doubtless offered some relief in these desperate conditions, but sadly they did little to turn the battle which these days is chiefly remembered for the brief but disastrous Charge of the Light Brigade. This resulted in 110 killed and another 160 wounded of the more than 600 men who had taken part on the British side. To these losses must be added a terrible total of 375 horses which were either killed in the action or deliberately destroyed shortly afterwards.

Despite this storied catastrophe, Britain somehow held on to the strategically important harbour but it was the Russians who claimed victory overall. They did so on the reasonable grounds that the positions they gained during the fighting severely hampered the progress of the siege and because they had also managed to capture a significant number of big British guns.

---

* Both paintings are in the collection of the Naval & Military Club in St James's Square, London.

Back in London no one queried the result and the authorities went so far as to award battle honours to those regiments which had taken part. This is something that rarely happens when a battle has been lost. The fact that it did is normally taken as official recognition that the failed charge was nevertheless an outstanding demonstration of personal courage, soldierly resilience and incredible determination.

This being so, it is somewhat sad that the subsequent history of the balaclava has done little to echo the honourable example of those men. The original balaclava was a simple, open-faced garment, but it was surprisingly versatile and could be quickly adapted by pulling it up to cover the mouth and chin, or indeed pulled down to protect just the neck. Variations have since appeared which cover the face completely, leaving only holes for the eyes and sometimes the mouth. In this form they have remained useful, and a black balaclava still forms an essential part of every SAS soldier's basic kit. Unfortunately, much the same is true of terrorists, paramilitaries, kidnappers, drug gangs and bank robbers, all of whom find the resulting anonymity an invaluable asset during the course of their own nefarious careers.

HOME OFFICE PATTERN HELMET

Now correctly known as the 'custodian helmet', the headgear of the average British bobby is surely so familiar that it really doesn't need another name.

The style has a long history of more than 150 years, although when the police first took to the streets of London in 1829 (only the Marine Police Force on the Thames is older) they did so wearing blue tail-coats and 'stovepipe' top hats with blue trousers for winter wear and white ones each summer. For a while inspectors were permitted to carry pistols, but constables, who had to be at least 5ft 7in, were allowed only a truncheon. This had a band of copper at one end and the Royal cipher at the other (WR, for William IV) and it is these which quickly gave rise to two enduring nicknames: Coppers and the Old Bill.

Their top hats might now seem an extraordinary choice, but it was far from accidental. Considerable thought went into what the men wore. Blue tunics were specified over red expressly to demonstrate that the new police were a civilian force rather than military one. This was an important distinction in Europe's age of revolution, but the authorities nevertheless recognised the importance of giving individual officers greater visibility on the street. They realised that this could most easily be achieved by issuing each man with a tall black hat.

The added height also lent the officers an air of greater authority but it had a more practical purpose too. The hats were made of beaver fur* with tough leather side pieces and a thick leather crown. Inside, a ring of wire and cane gave it surprising strength and rigidity. As well as protecting its wearer from a blow on the head, the greater rigidity meant the hat could be removed and placed on the ground whenever the constable

---

* Four carved stone beavers still sit above the façade of 105–109 Oxford Street in London. From 1822 this was a hat factory owned by Henry Heath. It was still operating in the 1930s and at its peak employed around seventy men and women working with felt made from the fur of beavers, otters, musk rats, rabbits and hares.

needed something to stand on in order to see what was happening on the other side of a tall fence or wall.

For all this, however, top hats were unlikely to remain the most practical choice of working headdress, and in 1863 the Met trialled an entirely new, bespoke helmet which was formally introduced two years later. The new design was reportedly influenced by the slightly ridiculous spike-topped *pickelhaub* worn by the Prussian army, but despite this it soon became an icon of Britishness. As familiar as the dome of St Paul's, it was later made even more famous by the avuncular, softly-spoken star of *Dixon of Dock Green*.

These first helmets were made of cork covered in dark felt or serge. This gave rise to yet another nickname for the hapless rozzers: Woodentop, which incidentally was the title of the 1983 forerunner of ITV's popular series *The Bill*. Their new domed shape was clearly going to be trickier than a top hat for anyone to stand on, but otherwise the design and construction offered many of the same advantages but at reduced cost.

Its superiority over the stovepipe was quickly recognised and it was soon adopted by county forces outside London, as well as by the police services of Canada, New Zealand, Monaco, Jordan, Samoa and even a handful of states in the US. In Italy white helmets were issued to officers directing the traffic, and for several years either side of the war something similar was worn by police in Brighton during the summer months.

Today the helmets are manufactured by a small number of specialist companies, two of which have been supplying the police since Victorian times. They are now made of tough, moulded plastic and still look much the same as P.C. Dixon's did in the 1950s although, like Tate & Lyle's famous golden syrup tin, the design has been subtly updated over the years.

The helmets also come in a variety of different styles, although superficially at least these all look much the same. The most distinctive is perhaps that worn by members of the City of London Police. This force is separate from the Met and its officers are charged with maintaining law and order inside the historic Square Mile and within the legal enclaves of Middle and Inner Temple.

Their helmet has changed less than most since its introduction in 1865. Instead of the Met's white metal boss it has the City of London's red and white coat of arms on the front, where other English and Welsh forces have a representation of St Edward's Crown and the eight- or sixteen-pointed Brunswick Star. The latter, incidentally, is a nod to Germany's Brunswick-Lüneburg region, a duchy ruled by King William's forebears at the time the Georgians replaced the Stuarts following the death in 1714 of Queen Anne. The Scots do not use it.

Both here and abroad, however, not every force has remained quite so loyal to the original Home Office Pattern helmet. Several UK constabularies have stopped using it altogether for cost or other reasons, and Scottish police haven't worn this sort of helmet since the 1950s. English officers do still wear them when on royal duties north of the border though, and it is interesting to see how many chief constables and police commissioners have made the decision to switch to baseball caps or flat hats or some other alternative only to then put his or her officers back into traditional helmets a few years later.

Peaked caps may be more fashionable. Perhaps they are easier to live with, and they are certainly better suited to those officers who spend all day in a police car or van. But it seems that for a constable doing his rounds on foot (ranks above sergeant don't wear them) the traditional Custodian still has a lot going for it.

For one thing, the aforementioned issue of height and visibility is still a live one, especially now that equality laws make it impossible to insist on a minimum height for officers of either sex.* The helmets are also instantly recognisable and, as has been shown numerous times, the larger size can be useful when it comes to protecting the modesty of streakers, male or female, at major sporting events. It could be argued that a baseball cap would do this last job just as well (who knows?) but one suspects one of these would never have won a starring role in the World Press Photo of the Year or the *Life Magazine* Picture of the Year.**

---

* At the time of writing, Britain's shortest policeman is a 1.5m tall boxer and martial arts enthusiast whose previous career in the army included spells in Iraq, Oman, Kuwait and Northern Ireland.
** Both of these awards were given to photojournalist Ian Bradshaw. In 1974 he took the most famous photograph of the naked Michael O'Brien 'wearing' PC Bruce Perry's helmet as he was escorted off the pitch during a rugby union friendly between England and France at Twickenham.

MÜLLER
CUT-DOWN

The strangest things get left on trains. Every year Transport for London's lost property department deals with more than 160,000 items which get left behind on trains, buses and the Tube. Not just books, bags and brollies either, but everything from outboard motors to a 14ft canoe, from glass eyes (plural) to inflatable dolls, from a box of stuffed bats to a bag containing two genuine human skulls.

A lot of this stuff eventually finds its way back to the right owners, usually courtesy of a computer programme which is nicknamed Sherlock because the division responsible for lost property is based in Baker Street. But not everyone is quite so lucky.

In 1919, for example, Colonel T.E. Lawrence forgot to pick up the copy of his memoirs which he'd been proofreading as he changed trains at Reading. No one handed it in and Lawrence had to rewrite the whole of *The Seven Pillars of Wisdom* from scratch, all 250,000 words of it. Even he might be considered lucky, however, compared to the owner of a distinctive gentleman's black beaver hat which hit the headlines after being mislaid in east London in 1864.

The hat in question was discovered on 9 July that year in a compartment of a North London Railway evening service running between the City and Chalk Farm. The compartment had recently been vacated by an elderly bank official called Thomas Briggs, but it wasn't his hat.

The unfortunate 69-year-old had been found lying by the side of the track after the driver of another train reported seeing something suspicious on the stretch between Victoria Park and Bow stations. He was badly injured and after being carried up the embankment and into a pub called the Mitford Castle,* the old man died of his injuries.

---

* This is located on Cadogan Terrace in Homerton and is now called the Top O'The Morning.

The first person in Britain to be murdered on a train, Briggs had also been robbed of a gold pocket watch and chain, his black top hat and a pair of spectacles. It looked like he'd been beaten up before being heaved out of the window of the moving train and it is assumed that his assailant jumped off before the service made its return journey to Fenchurch Street. It was on this return journey that two workers travelling back into town found a pool of blood, and the aforementioned black beaver hat.

The murder caused a sensation. The public were already a bit unsure about these newfangled railways. Things had got off to a shaky start when William Huskisson MP had been run down and killed by Stephenson's *Rocket*, and decades later many Londoners still thought trains were too fast and that passengers risked suffocating if they travelled at much more than walking pace. A brutal and bloody murder was the last thing the heavily indebted railway companies needed at this time, and soon an enormous £300 reward was offered for any information leading to an arrest.

The hat's owner, a 24-year-old German former gunsmith called Franz Müller, had been working in the area as a tailor. He decided to head for the United States, although there is still some confusion as to whether he was fleeing the scene of the murder or had simply committed the crime in order to pay for his passage. Either way, the police were quickly on his tail.

Publicity about the murder prompted a jeweller in Cheapside to come forward. The unfortunately named John Death claimed that a couple of days after the murder he had been offered a gold chain by a man with a strong German accent. Shortly afterwards the driver of a hackney carriage gave the police a photograph of Müller, who he said was a friend of his daughter's.

Death immediately identified him as the same man who had come into his shop and Müller was soon traced to an address in Bethnal Green. A warrant was issued for his arrest after a neighbour confirmed that he had talked of catching a ship sailing for America.

Two Scotland Yard detectives travelled to Liverpool and, in the hope that they could apprehend Müller before he disappeared to America, they boarded a fast steamship called the SS *City of Manchester*. Luck and technology were on their side. The wanted man had opted to travel by sail, which was much cheaper but also slower. Because of this, the detectives arrived more than two weeks ahead of Müller and were able to greet him as stepped ashore. The hapless German was arrested as soon as he stepped off the gangplank.

At the time the suspect was wearing a hat which was quickly identified as having belonged to Mr Briggs. This presumably explains why he had left his own at the scene. Later it turned out that he had spent some of his time at sea modifying it slightly, using his skills as a tailor to halve the height of the crown in order to produce a more fashionable profile.

The gold fob watch was also still in his possession and he was charged with murder. On returning to London he stood trial at the Old Bailey and was found guilty on the third day. Unusually, Kaiser Wilhelm II attempted to intercede on behalf of his subject, but, with the public (and the railway companies) clamouring for revenge, he was sentenced to be hanged on 14 November.

Executions at this time were still carried out in public. With the best seats selling for the equivalent of ten times a labourer's weekly wage, the crowd which gathered outside Newgate Prison numbered well over 30,000. Local pubs were doing an exceptionally brisk trade and the atmosphere soon turned from friendly to ugly. The resulting near-riot is now cited as one of the factors behind the decision a few years later to move all future executions to inside the prison walls.*

---

* The last public execution took place in London in May 1868, meaning that it was possible, if only for a few months, to travel by Underground railway to see a hanging, an uncomfortable coming-together of the modern and the medieval.

Müller's final words were '*Ja, iche habe es getan*' ('Yes, I did it') but the brutality of the murder left many Londoners genuinely horrified. The railway companies were encouraged to install some means of communication between individual carriages and the guard, but that wasn't the only legacy of this case. Extensive coverage of the murder, the thrilling nature of the transatlantic pursuit, and the riotous excitement surrounding Müller's execution also kick-started a strange millinery craze. Whether for reasons of style or because of his notoriety it is hard to tell, but the murderer's handiwork hit the spot and for several years afterwards the Müller Cut-Down was very much the hat to have.

Interestingly, Müller's headgear is by no means the only one to have featured in a violent crime. The nineteenth-century serial poisoner Thomas Neill Cream was identified by his black silk hat after killing several prostitutes, and in the 1960s, for the first time in a British criminal investigation, microscopic fibres found on a hat using ultraviolet light formed a key part of the forensic evidence used to convict a murderer.

Because of this there are several significant hats in the Crime Museum at Scotland Yard, as well as Müller's creepy death mask. These include the one worn by murdered WPC Yvonne Fletcher, who was gunned down in 1984 from the window of what was then the Libyan People's Bureau in St James's Square.** Also a floppy felt hat and balaclava disguise which belonged to one of the perpetrators of the Knightsbridge 'Spaghetti House Siege' in 1975.

** The hat lay on ground in the square during a ten-day standoff with the Libyans, until one of Fletcher's colleagues courageously took a chance and retrieved it.

HALLELUJAH BONNET

First seen in Britain in 1880, this was standard issue for women in the Salvation Army and remained so for nearly 100 years. The first of an initial batch of twenty-five was designed by a student at the Salvation Army school in east London, and made its debut on a march from Hackney to Whitechapel in celebration of the silver wedding of co-founders William and Catherine Booth.

The hat's designer, a milliner called Annie E. Lockwood, produced a straw and black silk version of the contemporary poke bonnet (also known as a Neapolitan). This was done in response to a personal request from Mrs Booth. The self-styled Army Mother wanted a hat for her soldiers to wear which was 'cheap, strong and large enough to protect the heads of the wearers from cold as well as from brick-bats and other missiles' thrown by those opposed to the organisation's Christian ethos.*

The bonnets cost 6s (30p) each and within a year the organisation had made them a compulsory part of the military-style uniform. This had been introduced a few years earlier by a reformed drunk called Elijah Cadman** and it quickly became a useful identifier for members doing good works in the slum districts of London and other big cities. The bonnets were soon a highly important symbol for the Salvation Army and one man recalled how it was only after his wife bought one of them that he realised she was serious about her faith: 'I threw my pipes, tobacco and pouch into the fire,' he said, 'gave up my glass, and got salvation for myself.'

---

* A newspaper account at the time records how members of the Salvation Army were considered 'fair game by the hooligans' and that their early open-air meetings 'were attacked by evil people whose interests were threatened'.

** The teenaged Cadman claimed he could 'fight like a devil and drink like a fish' but was converted to Christianity by a street preacher in Rugby whom he had gone to heckle.

Wearers in more than 100 countries were forbidden to make even slight alterations to Miss Lockwood's design, and when concerns were expressed that some younger cadets might not like the slightly crude design with its funereal black ribbons, Mrs Booth was adamant. 'If they have any complaints,' she stated, 'I'll just come and explain to them how important it is for us all to wear neat and plain bonnets that keep us safe and make us stand out as – Salvationists!'

This might suggest the hallelujah bonnets were unpopular, but by the 1920s they had managed to become admired fashion accessories among ordinary members of the public. It should be said that most civilians preferred their versions to be in colours other than the Salvation Army's flat black, and it's unlikely that any of them chose to be buried with their bonnets, which for many years was a Salvation Army tradition.

In February 1926 the *Manchester Guardian* reported that Parisians, no less, were switching to what it called 'Salvation Army Pokes' after tiring of wearing 'saucepans, paper-bags and sugar-loaves' on their heads. Evidently these were thought to be preferable to the so-called liberty cap or *bonnet rouge*, which for many French citizens was perhaps too reminiscent of the garments worn by those grisly old women, the *Tricoteuse*, who sat knitting in the shadow of the guillotine during the early years of the Revolution.

This particular fad appears to have been short-lived, however, although in 1938 a correspondent to *The Times* observed that interest in hallelujahs seemed to be growing again. This was as a result of a renewed taste for Victorian and Edwardian fashions which was said to be sweeping through Europe. In the end any thoughts of a revival were immediately squashed when Hitler marched into Poland.

Interestingly, there had been rumours that the Salvation Army might be looking for something different even earlier than this, but nothing came of these. In fact, the hallelujah bonnet was only retired towards the end of the 1970s, by which time its association with the organisation had become so strong that it had somehow ceased to look as old fashioned as it was. Various replacements have since been introduced which vary from country to country. Almost certainly none will last as long.

FEDORA

The original fedora took its name from a play, *Fédora*, by the French playwright Victorien Sardou. This was written for Sarah Bernhardt and was first performed in the United States in 1882. It tells the story of the hat-wearing, cross-dressing Princess Fédora Romazov and was later turned into an opera by Umberto Giordano and Arturo Colautti.

Numerous film adaptations followed (but not Billy Wilder's underrated 1978 classic of the same name, which is based on quite different source material) and the style of hat worn by Sardou's heroine, essentially a type of modified homburg (p.203), caught on almost immediately. At various times, unusually, it has been widely worn by both sexes.

Particularly in the United States, it was first worn as a symbol of the women's rights movement, although to modern eyes the more likely associations are with many famous Prohibition-era gangsters including Al Capone, 'Lucky' Luciano and 'Bugsy' Siegel. Humphrey Bogart wore one too as Rick Blaine in *Casablanca*, as did Indiana Jones. This switch away from suffragette fashion to testosterone-fuelled dynamo isn't as surprising as it at first seems. Much of the appeal of Bernhardt's character and her apparel conveyed her spirit of independence and assertiveness. Because of this her hat was always subtly suggestive of masculine undertones, so it was perhaps only a relatively small hop from Sardou's feisty heroine to the sometimes aggressive masculinity of its later wearers.

In Britain, Oscar Wilde was one of the first to wear the fedora. As early as 1883, Lock sold a black fedora to him ahead of a year-long speaking tour of the United States where he gave an impressive 140 public lectures. But with his silk stockings and flowing locks, Wilde was a famously flamboyant dresser – he also had a brown fedora, fully 6 inches tall – and as such very much an outlier.

In Britain the fashion for men in fedoras really only took off decades later in the 1920s, when the Prince of Wales, the future

Edward VIII, began wearing them. People forget this, however, and the prince is sometimes instead accused of hastening the decline in hat-wearing by arriving in Britain bareheaded after the death of his father in 1936. The future Poet Laureate John Betjeman captured the moment perfectly, describing how the heir to the throne arrived at Hendon aerodrome: 'The new suburb stretched beyond the runway, where a young man lands hatless from the air.'

The forward-looking prince was the first member of the Royal Family ever to fly in an aeroplane (a flimsy-looking Bristol F.2B fighter over the Italian front in September 1918) and his choice of dress must have been intentional. George V wore hats a lot but Edward, more or less permanently preoccupied with his appearance, may have been signalling his intention for his reign, short though it turned out to be, to be nothing like his father's.

Aside from in the cinema and the speakeasy, fedoras are still worn today, particularly by rabbis and other members of their Haredi and Orthodox communities. These tend to be black like Oscar Wilde's, although grey and brown have always been popular. 'Military' colours such a green, blue, maroon and khaki* also made a brief appearance in the 1940s but these are rarely seen now.

Similarly, while most fedoras are made of wool, cashmere, rabbit or beaver felt (felt is generally held to be far superior to wool) many other furs have been used including mink, mohair and chinchilla. Occasionally, similar hats have also been crafted from such rarities as vicuña and guanaco (both related to the Andean llama) and even cervelt, a luxurious fabric made from New Zealand red deer. As each of these animals produces just 20 grammes of raw material per year, the cost can be imagined.

---

* One of the many companies that encouraged this trend was Stetson, which gave its name to the cowboy's hat of choice, the celebrated 'Boss of the Plains'. The company still exists and has lent its name to a university and a law school, both of which founder John B. Stetson helped to establish.

Regardless of the raw materials used in manufacturing, the fedora is most easily distinguished from the homburg and the smaller, less showy trilby by its brim, which can be 6cm or even wider. Like its cousins it has a centre crease in its high (11cm) front-pinched crown and the brim can be stitched or trimmed or left 'raw'.

The hats are often lined and typically have a stitched cloth or leather sweatband inside and a broad ribbon around the outside. Occasionally the felt may be discreetly perforated to improve ventilation, and several manufacturers have advertised versions that can be rolled up without risk to the integrity of the shape. Given his oft-quoted declaration that 'one should either be a work of art, or wear a work of art', Oscar Wilde, one suspects, would very much have preferred cervelt to this particular innovation.

Although some of the most arresting images of Wilde show him wearing his famous black fedora, he never paid for it. It seems his account with its maker remained open during both of his trials and for as long as he was incarcerated in Pentonville, Wandsworth and finally Reading.* After this he exiled himself to Paris and the firm didn't pursue the debt, which at the time would have been considered an ungentlemanly thing to do.

Sadly, if hardly surprisingly, this admirable policy usually cost tailors and hat-makers dear. Winston Churchill's well-known penchant for acquiring many different types of military headgear and uniforms more than matched Mountbatten's and contributed to a series of enormous and long-running debts to Savile Row and St James's. In total these were equivalent to at least £30,000 in today's money, and throughout his life the great man's bills were only settled in the most relaxed manner.

---

* Only a few friends stuck by Wilde during his travails. When one of them, the novelist Ada Leverson, went to collect him from prison, he congratulated her on knowing 'exactly the right kind of hat to wear at seven o'clock in the morning to meet a friend who has been away'.

Because of this he was often five years or more in arrears and, perhaps in revenge for this, the journal *Tailor and Cutter* described his appearance at his marriage to Clementine Hozier in 1908 as 'one of the greatest failures as a wedding garment we have ever seen'.

In fact, in Wilde's case the final amount was only settled more than a century later. After reading about Lock's outstanding bill in *The Times*, a Wilde enthusiast from Worthing in Sussex decided to do the decent thing and sent a cheque to St James's Street to mark the centenary of his hero's death. Accompanied by an apology for the late payment, the Bank of Scotland cheque was made out for £3 6*s* 0*d* (£3.30), the cost in Wilde's day of a fedora, an opera hat (p.71) and a bowler.**

** Closer to our own, the *Raiders of the Lost Ark* fedora made £393,600 at auction, which is more than sixty times the price paid for the one worn by Michael Jackson in his 'Billie Jean' video.

MITRE

The earliest known illustrations of a bishop's mitre appeared in a Papal Bull nearly a thousand years ago, and in the exceptionally crowded field of liturgical costumes, it remains one of only a very few items that most Britons can identify by name. Despite its familiarity, however, it's unlikely that many realise how completely the mitre disappeared from churches in England during the Reformation or that the fashion for wearing them returned only towards the end of the nineteenth century.

The history of its name is both curious and convoluted. In Homer's *Iliad*, the word mitre refers to a broad, bronze waistband of the type warriors wore to protect their midriffs. It later came to be associated with headbands worn in Egypt and Babylon, and then later still with the sort of gorgeous, heavily jewelled closed crowns favoured by rulers of the Byzantine Empire.

By the mid-twelfth century a version of this had become normal wear for bishops and abbots of the Catholic Church, and the modern form had begun to take shape. At its simplest this comprised two identical stiff panels, each shaped a bit like inverted shields and stitched together at the sides. A pair of fringed streamers or ribbons, known as lappets, were hung from the back.

Inevitably, perhaps, a garment at first straightforward (if a little eccentric) quickly acquired a good deal of elaboration. Three distinct types were adopted by the Roman Catholic Church and these are still in use today.

The plain white linen or silk *simplex* is usually worn only at funerals and on Good Friday. The *auriphrygiata*, of plain gold cloth or white silk with gold or silver embroidery decoration, is reserved for penitential seasons, such as Advent and Lent. The last, the *pretiosa*, is frequently decorated with gold and precious stones and is worn for the principal Mass on feast days and most Sundays.

In the Anglican Church no such distinctions were made. Here mitres tended to be plainer and simpler, at least for 'ordinary' bishops* who were also granted right to place a mitre above their coat of arms if they had one. (This occupies the position where peers and knights display a helmet.) There have never been any formal rules about the hat's use in church, although one newly appointed bishop recalled how he was advised by an older hand, 'Don't pray with it and don't fuss with it.'

This was presumably an instruction to the bishop-designate to wear one during processions but to avoid repeatedly putting it on and then taking it off again throughout the service. This still sounds like good advice today, although, like many other aspects of worship that have become associated with 'High Church' ideas and Anglo-Catholicism, the mitre now appears to be falling out of favour once again.

In theory, each bishop retains the right to decide what to wear on most of the occasions at which he or she is expected to preside or participate, but this hasn't silenced calls to ban the mitre as the Church of England struggles to slow the decline in its congregations.

As the key figure in a ceremonial procession, or indeed when seated on his *cathedra* or throne, there is no doubt that a mitred bishop in full fig still makes a powerful symbol of Christian authority. Unfortunately, for some in the church, this vesting of authority in one person lies at the heart of the problem.

Priests, say the modernisers, should appear friendly and approachable, not majestic and remote. They also point out that such a statement of power and authority, almost by defini-tion, suggests a culture of deference, which in turn can make it hard for less-elevated priests and ordinary churchgoers to 'speak truth to power' when something goes wrong. More than a few of them also think these old-fashioned hats look a bit daft.

---

* The Archbishop of Canterbury often sports a highly decorated mitre of white, gold, blue and aquamarine. The Archbishop of York has an equally fancy item in emerald green, and a red and white mitre is granted to Hereford Cathedral's *Episcopus Puerorum* or boy-bishop, a chorister elected to this historic office for just one day of the year.

Needless to say, there are traditionalists who argue against this view, but they seem very much to be in the minority. They also know that, as much as they like them, mitre-wearing in Britain is more of a habit that a tradition (and not a very old one at that). There are those who insist the hat's origins go all the way back to the *mitznefet* or turban worn by High Priests in the Old Testament, but these guys weren't even Christian and anyway, the link between the two is far from certain.

In fact, the only certainty is that no Church of England bishop wore a mitre until 1885. The first to do so was Edward King,* who adopted the practice when he was named Bishop of Lincoln. But frankly he's an awkward role model for anyone. If King is remembered at all, it's only because he was accused of conspiring in 'ritualistic practices'. These probably weren't as sinister as they sound, but nevertheless my Lord Bishop was found guilty and, despite an attempt to duck the embarrassment of a regular public trial (by swearing in a special archiepiscopal court, which hadn't sat for more than 200 years), the verdict caused a scandal.

---

* His nephew Robert King followed him into the priesthood but also played football for England. He was on the winning side when Ireland lost 13–0 at Bloomfield Park in Belfast in 1882. This is still a record score for an England team, although the fact that the Football League still uses 'Mitre' footballs is almost certainly a coincidence.

STRAW BOATER

Forever associated with Jerome K. Jerome's 1889 bestseller *Three Men in a Boat*,* the straw boater has long been a hat for the summer months and has an air of fun to it, despite having formed a part of the uniforms of many schools in Britain and abroad. Most obviously it came to be associated with rowing and punting and other means of 'messing about on the river', although East End costermongers also wore them and Herbert Hoover managed somehow to wear his while driving his open-top Panhard without it flying off. This was during the six years the prospective US president spent living in England, commuting between an apartment in London's Hyde Park Gate and a weekend home in Surrey (called, curiously enough, The White House).

Today the most famous boaters are probably those worn by the boys of Harrow School in north-west London, although the same hats play an important role – for one day a year, at least – at its rival Eton's traditional Fourth of June celebrations. The day sees parents looking up from their picnics on Agar's Plough, as Collegers and Oppidans stand in their boats and raise dozens of flower-adorned boaters in salute. After cheering the Queen, the school and the memory of George III, the boys shake the flowers off into the Thames.**

It's a charming sight, although one of the unfortunate results of this harmless bit of private pageantry, in Britain at least, has been to transform the blameless boater from an elegant and unisex item of leisurewear into a potent symbol of privileged social status and the supposed inequality of life. It won't have

---

* *To Say Nothing of the Dog.* The book's popularity has never really dimmed but readers still overlook the fact that the full title includes a reference to little Montmorency who accompanies the three companions on their voyage.
** The date is the birthday of King George III. The 'Kynge's College of Our Ladye of Eton besyde Windesore' was founded in 1440 by Henry VI but King George III was a frequent and popular visitor. He spent much of his time at Windsor during his long reign and invited many of the boys to visit him at the castle for tea.

helped that so many of the boys' fathers arrived to watch the event in top hats until at least the Second World War.

Italy has no such problem (in Venice the hat is part of every gondolier's apparel) and in the USA too the associations seem entirely different. Across the Atlantic examples of what they call the skimmer are most commonly worn by barbershop quartets, tap dancers and other Vaudeville types, usually at a jaunty angle and often with sleeve garters and striped vests or waistcoats.

In the 1930s boaters were also popular with agents working for the FBI, and another skimmer makes a famous appearance towards the end of the 1969 film *Butch Cassidy and the Sundance Kid*. After spotting the distinctive plain white hat on a Bolivian street corner, the duo realise it belongs to their relentless pursuers, the so-called super posse headed by the lawman Joe Lefors and a mysterious Native-American tracker who calls himself 'Lord Baltimore'.

Skimmer is only one of many names applied to the straw boater. Maurice Chevalier's was a *canotier* and the hats are also known as bashers, katies, straw-sailors, somers, and in Japan, *suruken* or *can-can* hats. Although its original creator is unknown, the first boaters were almost certainly British. It's probably also the case that they were manufactured in Luton, the historical centre of English millinery and for the last 100 years home to what is now this country's only surviving boater maker.***

The earliest designs may have been modified versions of a type of French sailor's hat. Then as now, they were made of plaited sisal or sennit straw, which is coiled and then moulded into a flattened pillbox shape with a wide, flat brim. The finished item turns out to be light and surprisingly tough, if not quite indestructible.

*** The town's museum has a collection of more than 700 hats spanning three centuries or more. Historic hat-making machinery can also be seen in action at the Hat Works Museum in Stockport.

The flat crown is traditionally ringed by a band of grosgrain or corded ribbon which can be of a solid colour although more often it is striped. A striped ribbon means the hat can be readily personalised to advertise the wearer's affiliation to a particular club, college, regiment or university – or indeed a school. Unsurprisingly this has proved to be an irresistible attraction, and not just in Britain.

Of course, every hat has its heyday, and the boater's was impressively long. Its simple, clean lines made it immensely popular from the 1880s to the mid 1930s, but after this it was gradually supplanted by more elaborate shapes, such as the panama and trilby. The decline led to boaters being thought of more and more as school attire, and this in turn probably turned older wearers against them, thereby accelerating their decline still further.

For schools, however, the boater still seemed to have a lot going for it. Less formal and more affordable than a top hat, it was special in a way the ubiquitous school cap was not. Because of this (it was hoped) it reflected well on both schools and their pupils.

That was the theory anyway, but of course caps were common because they were far more practical. School boaters tended to be shallower than the adult versions, and being bought off-the-peg, they rarely if ever fitted the wearers' heads properly, which made them look odd and feel uncomfortable.

Worse still, literally any school hat makes an irresistible target for boys from rival institutions, but the flat, stiff frisbee-like shape of the boater was just asking to be snatched off and thrown (or 'skimmed') over the nearest hedge or under a passing car. Little wonder so many boaters were ritually burnt once the holidays arrived (or flung under buses by those forced to wear them). No surprise either that schools finally began phasing them out in the 1970s.

It wasn't just misbehaving schoolboys that did for the boater though. More than most, it fell victim to the general decline in hat-wearing. When almost everyone in Britain wore hats – grown-ups and children, and regardless of class – the boater was just one among many. But once hats began to slip out of fashion, it rapidly became more of a stage prop, something nostalgic, almost a joke. For a while, slightly bizarrely, the straw boater was adopted by the once mighty John Player Team Lotus F1 team as part of its official uniform, but few people wear them now, except to make a point. All of which is fine, but what was once fashion has been demoted to little more than fancy dress.

DUNCE CAP

Definitely the hat no one wants to wear if he wishes to get ahead, the conical white dunce's hat was a familiar form of punishment in Victorian times, a less kindly age when reluctant pupils at schools in Britain and North America were made to sit or stand facing the corner of the classroom.

Deliberately humiliating anyone in this way who, to take the accepted definition of a dunce, is 'incapable of learning,' seems harsh if not actually idiotic, but then the origin of the word dunce is itself a little tangled – and older than one might imagine.

The name is commonly held to derive from that of John Duns (c.1266–1308), more commonly known as Duns Scotus. As a philosopher and theologian, he was recognised during his lifetime as a great metaphysical thinker and he is still regarded as one of the leading intellectuals of the High Medieval period.

Duns travelled widely to lecture at schools and universities in Oxford, Paris and Cologne and as such he doesn't seem like an obvious candidate for the role of dimwit. Unfortunately his reputation, like that of many other long-dead Catholic intellectuals, took a dive during the English Reformation. As the Church of England took steps to break away from Rome in the sixteenth century, the term *duns* or dunce seems to have become a popular term of abuse, at least among Protestant agitators. It was used to describe anyone they considered foolish or incapable of scholarship and these jibes continued when the philosopher's supporters, known as Scotists, showed their determination to argue forcefully against the tenets and principles of Renaissance Humanism.

It should be said that not everyone accepted this sad reversal in the philosopher's fortunes, or by extension the word's origins; the lexicographer Dr Johnson admitted only that these were obscure. Many ecclesiastical academics and the senior churchmen similarly continued to hold Duns and his writings in high regard long after his death* and some Catholics still refer to him as Doctor Subtilis ('the Subtle Doctor') in acknowledgment of the many subtle distinctions and nuances present in his writings.

Whatever the real answer, it is by no means a simple or straightforward line that links Professor Duns to the word dunce and to the conical hat of humiliation. The truth is that not much is known about the man himself as opposed to his work, although this hasn't been enough to prevent some self-declared authorities from drawing attention to a theory he is said to have advanced suggesting that conical or pointed hats somehow 'funnelled' knowledge into the wearer's brain.

Even without much understanding of neurological processes, common sense surely suggests that to do this a hat would need to be inverted. It is true that an apex (or point) could conceivably be seen as the summit of knowledge. It has been noted that wizards and witches wear pointy hats – at least in fairy tales – and that they are often supposed to have been wise men and women rather than mischievous, green-skinned pantomime villains. Victims of the Spanish Inquisition were also made to wear so-called steeple-crowned hats, usually immediately before being burned at the stake.

All that said, it was true nevertheless that countless portraits of Duns show him wearing a tall *domed* hat (or no hat at all) and that it is hard, if not impossible, to find an image of him wearing a pointed cone. Whatever the truth of this, the insult, once coined, has proved hard to shift, and the hat with or without a prominent 'D' on the front somehow followed on behind.

By 1624 a play by John Ford and Thomas Decker called *The Sun's Darling* featured something called a dunce-table, at which dullards and less-able children were seated apart from

---

* Having already been declared 'Venerable', Duns was beatified by Pope John Paul II in 1993, so the Blessed John must now be assumed to be on the path towards becoming St John at some future date.

their classmates. Similarly, in 1841, Charles Dickens in *The Old Curiosity Shop* described a classroom in which a dunce's cap is set on a shelf on its own. This, the author writes, is made from 'old newspapers and decorated with glaring wafers of the largest size'. That he doesn't waste any time describing what the cap is for, or who gets to wear it, suggests the concept was by then well understood by the average reader in Victorian England.

Indeed, it seems most likely that it was during precisely this period that the dunce's hat or cap really came into its own. Presumably in the same way that those charged with educating the young believed (or affected to believe) that it was possible to 'beat some sense' into a recalcitrant pupil with a cane, the idea took hold – and spread far and fast – that class clowns were best served by being made to wear a silly hat whilst standing facing the corner along with the slow learners, the lazy, the inattentive and the downright disruptive.

The whole notion seems slightly childish now, and how extraordinary that such a practice should have been maintained until so late into the twentieth century. Quite when the hats finally began to disappear is hard to say, but it took until 2010 for a number of education authorities in the UK to issue formal guidelines after concerns were voiced that the habit of sending a small child to the 'dunce's corner' might actually breach his or her human rights.

So far, so good, but even these didn't prevent protests a full two years later when the father of a Nottinghamshire schoolboy objected to his 8-year-old being made to wear a fluorescent hi-vis jacket as a punishment for misbehaving. It didn't have a large 'D' on the back, but even so …

DEERSTALKER

The subject of fifty-six short stories and four novels by Sir Arthur Conan Doyle (1859–1930) – and seemingly numberless adaptations for screen and stage – Sherlock Holmes is as closely associated with the deerstalker as Chaplin and his bowler or Her Majesty the Queen and the Imperial State Crown (p.207). There is, even so, scant evidence in the canonical works to suggest that Holmes wore such a thing more than once or twice.

In 'The Adventure of the Silver Blaze', Dr Watson describes Holmes as wearing 'his ear-flapped travelling cap' but the word deerstalker is never used, and nothing else we know about the world's most famous fictional detective suggests that such a garment would have formed part of his regular wardrobe.

Holmes, indeed, is depicted by his creator as a mostly conventionally attired, acutely fashion-conscious urbanite. A top hat therefore seems far more likely, although Conan Doyle actually mentions his clothes only very rarely. Nor do we know much about his appearance, except that he was rather more than 6ft tall and meticulously groomed, with a hawk-like nose, black hair and grey eyes.

For actors portraying him on stage or screen, and for the stories' early illustrators, it wasn't much to go on. Because of this, it seems likely that one of those given the task of representing Holmes on the page came up with the idea of dressing him in a deerstalker as a way of creating a distinctive and more memorable appearance for Conan Doyle's rising star.

The guilty party in this case was a commercially successful illustrator called Sidney Paget,* who produced an illustration of Holmes and Watson sharing a railway compartment in 'The Boscombe Valley Mystery'. When the story was published in *The Strand Magazine* in 1891, its readers were presented with an image of Watson dressed as one would expect for a

---

* Two of Paget's brothers, Henry Marriott and Walter Stanley, were also successful artists. It has been suggested that Sidney's version of Holmes was based on one of them, but the illustrator always denied this.

professional man of the period. Sitting opposite him in the carriage, Holmes is shown in a more eye-catching rig that includes the soon-to-be-famous deerstalker and an Inverness Cape.

In fact, Conan Doyle dressed his hero in an Ulster, an overcoat rather than a cape, but Paget's admittedly handsome invention struck a chord that resonated. In an early American stage adaptation of one of the stories, actor William Gillette similarly reached for a deerstalker, presumably to ensure that his character would be instantly recognisable. Gillette is also thought to have been responsible for introducing the detective to his now-familiar curved or calabash pipe. In the books Holmes always had a preference for straight stems.

This new version of Holmes quickly crossed back across the Atlantic and today it is the accepted one not just in Britain but around the world. Before long it no longer mattered that the 'real' Holmes would almost certainly have worn a black top hat or a bowler. When a prominent bronze statue was erected close to his creator's birthplace in Edinburgh, it showed him looking as people want him to look – dressed in a cape and deerstalker, with a calabash in his hand.

Yet without this connection, one wonders if the deerstalker would still exist today, and if anyone would still recognise one. Stalking has only ever been a minority sport, even in the Highlands, and its customs and complexities are obscure except to the few who do it. Stalkers may insist it is an ancient craft (and it is) but even most Scots still don't really understand what it involves. Few care what goes into a 'piece' and fewer still want to know how to spy, hardle, gralloch or drag.

By the same token it is hard to imagine that, without Holmes, many people would give much thought to the sport's traditional garb. Aside from the fact that many modern stalkers don't wear them, the hat's style is strangely maladapted for any situation away from the knoll or the corrie so it makes an unlikely fashion accessory.

Traditionally the hats were made of patterned woollen tweed, although examples have been produced in cotton canvas or duck and even suede. The distinguishing features are the same, either way: a pair of stiffened semi-circular bills or visors, front and rear, and a pair of soft earflaps which are usually worn fastened up around the sides of the hat with ribbons.

To its defenders this is still the ideal, the hat for all seasons. The peak-like visors protect both the neck and the face from sunburn, which is important because a day's stalking, successful or otherwise, will usually involve spending many hours on exposed hillsides. The earflaps similarly come into their own in bad weather, while a patterned tweed is said to provide the best possible camouflage (deer are very easily spooked), although this same patterning is also said, slightly paradoxically, to make it easier for stalkers to spot each other, thereby minimising the risk of accidents.

Whatever the truth of this point, it seems unlikely that anyone today would pick a heavy woollen hat to provide protection from the sun, or choose lightweight earflaps when heavy weather is closing in. Prime Minister Harold Macmillan's well-known preference for tweed plus-fours and a deerstalker was already regarded as a bit of an affectation more than half a century ago, especially when he wore them on a trip to a Soviet collective in Kiev.* But somehow none of this seems to matter: deerstalkers are still made and bought and worn, and it is hard to think that anyone but Sidney Paget should take the credit.

As for Holmes, it's unlikely that anyone would dare to replace his deerstalker, not now and not if they've seen what happens when people tinker with a winning formula. In 1893, when another of Paget's brilliant illustrations showed the

---

* In fact, Macmillan's appearance was regarded as eccentric even on the grouse moor, although he was a keen shot and kept it up until well into his eighties.

detective falling to his death at the Reichenbach Falls, readers of *The Strand* were genuinely outraged.

Hundreds wrote letters of complaint to the editor and the cancellation of more than 20,000 subscriptions threw the future of the magazine into doubt almost overnight. Conan Doyle was roundly condemned by fans and staff alike. All this may sound like just another day on the Internet, but in late-Victorian England calling anyone but a convicted criminal 'you brute' was tantamount to a personal attack. Conan Doyle's response was to surrender and Sherlock Holmes duly reappeared intact and unharmed – and almost certainly, if a little improbably, dressed in a deerstalker.**

** *The Strand Magazine* recovered and survived until 1950. Its final editor was Macdonald Hastings, father of the journalist and historian Max Hastings.

TRILBY

The publication in 1894 of the novel *Trilby* was a phenom-
enal success for the author George du Maurier and his USA
sales alone accounted for more than 200,000 copies. Today,
its plot largely forgotten, the book is mostly remembered for
introducing the character of Svengali. This highly manipula-
tive hypnotist and musician exercises a sinister hold over the
book's eponymous heroine, a half-Irish artists' model called
Trilby O'Farrell.

Du Maurier's book was turned into a ballet and there have
been numerous film versions in the years since, including
one with a female Svengali (played by Jodi Foster) and several spoofs. However, it is the 1895 stage adaptation by the
American playwright Paul M. Potter that really concerns us
here, for it was the West End production that launched the now
famous hat of the same name. It was produced and directed by
the actor-manager Herbert Beerbohm Tree, who also took the
role of Svengali.

Tree knew of the novel and sent his half-brother, the humour-
ist Max Beerbohm, to see the play in Boston. Max reported back
from America that the story was 'absolute nonsense'. He was
convinced the play would fall flat in London but, after seeing
it for himself, Beerbohm Tree disagreed and rushed to secure
the British rights. The first performances were at Manchester's
Theatre Royal and a matter of weeks later it transferred to the
Haymarket Theatre in central London.

Although Max still refused to change his opinion of the play
more than sixty years later, the play was a huge hit, like the book
had been. Incredibly, Herbert – later Sir Herbert – was able to
build a completely new theatre using his share of the profits.*
Once again it was the heroine's headgear that caught the eye of

---

* Her Majesty's Theatre, also in Haymarket, was actually the fourth
playhouse on this Crown Estates site. For a year it provided a lavish
Louis XV-style home for the new (Royal) Academy of Dramatic Art,
which Beerbohm Tree founded in 1904.

the audience (see Fedora, p.139) although very few trilby wearers nowadays give even a moment's thought to Miss O'Farrell. Not many play-goers do either, for that matter: in the long run she has proved to be nowhere near as memorable as Svengali.

The structure of the hat is similar to a fedora, although the smaller trilby has a shorter, slightly sharper crown and, most importantly, a narrower brim. The latter is angled down at the front and slightly turned up at the back. To begin with, felt trilbies were very much a bohemian accessory (tweed versions only began appearing later) but it is now regarded as rather smart.

Initially its more relaxed style was welcomed as a move away from the uncompromising formality of the Victorians' black silk top hat. Several writers and artists attached to the Bloomsbury Group were frequently seen wearing them, and the poet and painter Isaac Rosenberg (1890–1918) put one on for the two self-portraits that now hang at Tate Britain and in the National Portrait Gallery.

By the 1930s, however, the trilby had begun to move upmarket, and brown ones especially became firm favourites among members of the racing fraternity. Racehorse owners, trainers and other lovers of the Turf still buy quantities of them today, in recognition of which many of those sold by Lock & Co. bear the names of famous courses, such as Wetherby, Sandown, Chepstow, Pickering and Haydock.

The journey from Edwardian Bloomsbury to the realm of Byerley Turk was not a straight route, however. Unfortunately there was also a time when trilbies appealed to the criminal classes – think Pinkie Brown and his gang in Graham Greene's *Brighton Rock*, or *Minder*'s Arthur Daley – but also to many influential musicians including Sinatra, Dylan, Leonard Cohen, Keith Richard and both of the Blues Brothers, although theirs were custom made and may have been fedoras.**

** For musicians with slightly less influence the trilby has also proved itself the perfect receptacle for collecting coins on the Underground.

Hilary Alexander, fashion director of *The Daily Telegraph,* recently cited the example of one British department store buyer she knows who insisted that, 'every time Van Morrison goes on stage, the loudest cheers will undoubtedly come from hat manufacturers across the world.' Based on his own experience, he told Ms Alexander, the Northern Irish musician was at least in part responsible for a healthy '105% leap' in trilby sales over a two-year period. Other celebrity trendsetters, such as Kate Moss, Johnny Depp and Keira Knightley, can presumably also take a share of the credit, although trilbies worn by the likes of Enoch Powell and Jeremy Thorpe may have had the opposite effect.

While it's true that fewer ordinary people now wear them, it's not hard to discern the benefits of a trilby. Whether fur-felt or tweed, they are warm, comfortable and showerproof but also sometimes crushable and compact enough and familiar enough not to attract too much attention. Unlike Beau Brummel's hat, they are also easy enough to raise an inch to an acquaintance spotted across the street – and, as *Country Life* once observed, a trilby is just the thing for hailing a cab.

CHEF'S TOQUE

Britain's first celebrity chef is generally assumed to be Alexis Soyer (1810–58), who invented spotted dick, attempted to reverse the Great Irish Famine of the 1840s and went on to earn the equivalent of £3 million a year in the kitchens of the Reform Club. Auguste Escoffier (1846–1935) ran him a close second, however. The son of a blacksmith, he spent seven years cooking in the army before following in his fellow Frenchman's footsteps to London. There he joined forces with César Ritz, the Swiss manager of the new and luxuriously appointed Savoy Hotel.

It is generally supposed that it was Escoffier's army background that enabled him so successfully bring almost military precision to the creation of complex French dishes. Instilling a sense of order and discipline throughout the hotel's kitchens, he organised his staff into a rigid hierarchy and worked hard to train the platoon to ensure that everything ran like clockwork night and day.

It worked too. The Savoy was an almost instant success, and before long guests could see an important social development taking place under its roof. For the first time in London, according to the chef's entry in the *Dictionary of National Biography*, aristocratic ladies, hitherto largely unaccustomed to dining in public, were now to be 'seen in full regalia in the Savoy dining and supper rooms'.

As well as bringing in more efficient working practices, Escoffier introduced a number of significant new dishes during his time at the hotel. These included the famous *Pêche Melba* in honour of the Australian singer Nellie Melba,* a flaming ice called the *Bombe Néro* and the delightful sounding *Fraises à*

---

* To celebrate the diva's visit to London in 1893, the chef combined her favourite ingredients (peaches, raspberries, redcurrant jelly and vanilla ice cream) in such way as to reduce the impact of the cold ice cream on her priceless vocal cords. The dish made its debut at a dinner Ms Melba was hosting at the hotel, where it was presented in an ice sculpture of a swan as a nod to her appearance in Wagner's Lohengrin at Covent Garden.

la Sarah Bernhardt which brought together strawberries, fresh pineapple and Curaçao sorbet.

Another of his innovations was the toque blanche, which had not been seen in Britain before. Professional cooks in this country had been wearing hats for centuries, it is sometimes said because Henry VIII beheaded one of them after finding a stray hair in his dinner. But Escoffier wasn't interested in the merely practical and saw the toque as the crowning glory of the neat, spotless and starched uniforms which 'the king of chefs and the chef of kings' now insisted everyone working under him should wear.

The word toque is simply Breton for hat, but Escoffier hailed from the Alpes-Maritimes region hundreds of miles further south so there was nothing of the Brittany peasant in this new version.

By any standards it was a quite extraordinary item. Its considerable height was intended to signify the wearer's rank or position within the Savoy kitchen hierarchy, and those worn by the more senior members of the team grew so tall they had to be reinforced with cardboard. Similarly the number of pleats let into the fabric – which could be as many as 100 – was supposedly an indication of the chef's skill and the sophistication of his cooking techniques.

In this case skill seems to have been measured by the number of different ways someone could prepare an egg, although thinking about this it seems unlikely that anyone would have been issued with a new hat every time he perfected another recipe. Whatever the truth of the matter, it is easy to see that as toques grew taller and taller they risked becoming less and less practical. Before long, one suspects, the whole thing must have begun to look like what it was – an elaborate piece of theatre.

Not that anyone would have accused Escoffier of merely showing-off – by the standards of the time he was definitely something of a genius – but his career at the Savoy nevertheless came to a sudden and shuddering halt when he and Ritz were sacked for gross negligence in 1898.

Unsurprisingly, their dismissal caused an uproar in the West End and some extraordinary scenes were described in the press as police officers attempted to wrestle the pair out of the hotel past a phalanx of 'sixteen fiery French and Swiss cooks', several of whom had armed themselves with long knives and 'placed themselves in a position of defiance'.

Eventually it took the best part of a day to get Ritz, Escoffier and a third man out of the building, and the trio soon afterwards announced that they would be suing the hotel owner for wrongful dismissal. Instead, after much legal toing and froing, all three went on to sign confessions in which they admitted committing a string of criminal offences.

Specifically, an astonishing £6,377 worth of alcohol had been spirited out of the hotel over a period of six months. This had been resold by the gang and numerous friends and shady business contacts had been accommodated at the hotel free of charge. M. Escoffier further admitted that he had accepted gifts and bribes from hotel suppliers which he agreed totalled 5 per cent of the value of everything coming into the kitchens.

The Frenchman eventually accepted that he was liable to repay £8,000 to his erstwhile employer, although in the end Richard D'Oyly Carte generously agreed to accept just £500 because Escoffier had already spent his ill-gotten gains. Altogether the hotel managed to recoup a total of £19,137 from the gang, equivalent to around £2.4 million today – to put it into some kind of perspective, this was only a few hundred pounds short of the Savoy's entire profits for the year.

Despite the signed admissions of larceny, embezzlement and serious fraud – and clear evidence that the three had been at it for years – none of this ever came to court. Nor, incredibly, do the careers of the three seemed to have suffered unduly despite the scale of their crimes. Escoffier immediately went off with his Swiss friend to found the Paris Ritz, and a few years later they opened a sister branch in London as a rival for the Savoy.

SLOUCH HAT

Despite its somewhat casual name, the slouch hat is an item of military headgear. They were common throughout the British Empire towards the end of the Victorian era but were not a British invention. Similar hats had long been worn by both Union and Confederacy troops in North America,* as well as in France, Austria and Germany. In Australia they were known as diggers and, after becoming inextricably bound up with that country's founding myths of rugged stockmen and 'swaggies' wandering the outback, they are now an important icon of the army.

The British authorities began issuing their own version to troops during the bloody and controversial Second Boer War (1899–1902). The name was a reference to the way in which only one side of the brim was pinned up leaving the other to 'slouch' downwards. This was done to enable the wearer to carry a rifle over one shoulder, as we saw earlier with the seventeenth-century tricorne.

Something similar had already been worn by at least one Scottish regimental pipe band, but the issuing of slouch hats to British troops fighting in South Africa is thought to have been authorised only because traditional cork and pith helmets (p.97) were in short supply. This new hat offered similar excellent protection from dazzling sunlight and prolonged downpours, but was also crushable, making it easy to stow.

Determined to defeat the Boers, Britain eventually fielded an overwhelming force of more than 500,000 men, but not all of them were issued with the new-style hats. Those who got them tended to be recent recruits to newly formed units rather than members of the regular army, whose commanding officers may have been more resistant to change.

---

* Where a version is known as the hardee or Jeff Davis hat after the Secretary of War who first authorised its use. President Theodore Roosevelt was probably its most famous wearer, having adopted it in the 1890s during his time as a commander of cavalry in the Spanish-American War. John Wayne also wore one when he wasn't in a Stetson.

These new units included the City of London Imperial Volunteers, the Imperial Yeomanry and its offshoot the King Edward's Horse. Interestingly, the last-named comprised four separate companies called the British Asian, British African, British American (i.e. Canadian) and Australasian squadrons. These recruited only foreign subjects living in or near London,** although the British side also included a further 100,000 African auxiliaries who were recruited locally. In recognition of the squadrons' unusual make-up, the force was subsequently renamed King Edward's Horse (The King's Overseas Dominions Regiment) and acquitted itself honourably during the Great War.

It seems reasonable to suppose, however, that the hats were never that popular even with these volunteers. They were rejected by the army at the first opportunity and when standardised khaki service dress was introduced a couple of years later, peaked service caps became the norm. The Royal East Kent Mounted Rifles retained their slouch hats for a bit longer, but this was unusual and they wore them mostly for ceremonial duties. A version nicknamed the 'lemon squeezer' is also worn by troops in New Zealand.

The only other exception seems to have been the 2nd Gurkha Rifles who began wearing something very similar on the North-Western Frontier in 1901. Their *terai* (named after a region in Nepal) is made of multiple layers of cloth and covered with a type of local tweed called 'puttoo'. A light muslin *puggaree* or scarf shields the wearer's neck from the sun, and ventilating holes and chin straps complete what has become known, in modern army quartermaster parlance, as 'Hats, Felt, Gurkha'.

Except for these, the slouch hat had more or less disappeared by 1910, but then it resurfaced a few years later in Ireland, where similar hats were spotted on many of those taking part in the failed 1916 Easter Rising. These afterwards became the

---

** As the fighting dragged on, this was extended to include residents of Oxford, Cambridge and Liverpool.

subject of a popular revolutionary song called *The Broad Black Brimmer* ('with ribbons frayed and torn'), which makes several references to the ad hoc uniforms worn by members of the original Irish Republican Army.

The legitimate army, meanwhile, really only took to the slouch again in the 1940s during the Burma Campaign. This saw an Allied force nearly a million strong facing troops from Japan and its puppet regimes in Thailand and India. Memories of the battles that followed, and the continuing Gurkha connection, mean that slouch hats are more likely to be associated in the public imagination with the terrible rigours of jungle warfare rather than the dust and scorched earth of the former Orange Free State.

PANAMA

The panama's popularity in the West is often put down to a canny piece of public relations on the part of the twenty-sixth President of the United States of America, but its success really began more than half a century earlier during the California Gold Rush of 1848–55.

In 1906, during a visit to inspect construction work on the new Panama Canal, Theodore Roosevelt was photographed sitting astride a giant steam shovel wearing (what else?) a panama hat. This had almost certainly been made in Ecuador – the best ones still are – but the president was keen to publicise the vast engineering enterprise which had recently passed into American hands from its original French instigators. To underline his political and commercial coup, the president cheerfully took advantage of the long-running confusion over the hat's name and its origins.

Hats like these had been woven and worn in Ecuador's coastal provinces of Guayas and Manabí for centuries. Locally they were known as *jipijapa* or *toquilla* and later as *Montecristi* after the town where the first factory was established to manufacture the hats for export. Before 1835 most of the hats had been produced in the region's villages by small-scale artisans, a classic cottage industry. The factory's Spanish owner, Manuel Alfaro y González, had much bigger ideas and spotted a huge commercial opportunity in America's first real gold rush.

Alfaro was confident he could supply literally tens of thousands of miners and prospectors with stylish, lightweight hats as they travelled up the Atlantic coast on their way to fortune or more likely failure. Streamlining production and employing only the most skilled weavers, he began shipping large quantities of hats from local ports to the Isthmus of Panama, where sales rocketed as more and more gold-diggers passed through.

This success meant the hats eventually became Ecuador's largest single export. Panama-mania made a fortune for Alfaro but unfortunately it also meant that – much like Stilton cheese in Britain* – the hats themselves became ineradicably linked in the common mind with the place of sale rather than their place of manufacture.

The revenues from hat sales nevertheless transformed Ecuador's primitive economy and made it possible for Alfaro's son to quit commerce and go into politics. José Eloy Alfaro eventually served two terms as the country's president and is now credited with modernising Ecuadorian society by overhauling the education system, rejecting religious superstitions, and radically improving public transport and communication.

In 1925 another great political moderniser, Turkey's Mustafa Kemal Atatürk, chose to put on a panama when he dressed himself in a Western three-piece suit and banned his country's traditional red fez. This looks like a wise choice for, although it is sometimes derided as just another straw hat, the genuine South American article really is something special.

A popular legend has it that when the first of Alfaro's countrymen arrived in Ecuador in the sixteenth century, the *conquistadors* were so transfixed by the beauty of the natives' glossy, translucent headdresses that they assumed these must have been woven using the fine skins of young vampire bats.

In reality the Incas constructed their headgear using fibres harvested from the *Carludovica palmata*. This is a palm-like plant found throughout the Americas and known locally as *Paja Toquilla*. Once boiled and dried, its fibres are soft, flexible and durable, and can be woven into hats which are light and breathable but strong. The Incas designed their hats without brims, however. The modern style worn by Christie's Poirot, Robert Redford's Great Gatsby and Gregory Peck in *To Kill a Mockingbird* evolved much later.

---

* Beginning in the 1720s this was made in Leicestershire, but took its name from a village on the Great North Road from where it was transported to London.

It seems likely that a few gold prospectors took their hats back to Europe (if not their shirts), but the fashion for panamas really only took off here and became a summer staple after examples had gone on display at the Exposition Universelle in Paris in 1855.

Like the Great Exhibition in London four years earlier, this was a mammoth affair and attracted more than 5 million visitors to its 40-acre site. Among the thousands of exhibitors was Phillipe Raimondi, a Frenchman resident in Panama who had travelled back to France with several hats made in Montecristi. One of these was offered to Napoleon III, Bonaparte's nephew, who naturally visited the Exposition several times. There are alas no surviving images of the emperor actually wearing his hat, but the connection proved invaluable and before long more than half a million hats a year were crossing the Atlantic from the thriving new port at Guayaquil.

Then as now, many different terms were bandied about to describe the quality of one panama relative to another, far more of them it seems than with any other type of hat. Needless to say, most of these were effectively meaningless: there has never been an independent governing authority; no one in any official position assays panama hats for quality.* It has, however, always been the case that the cost of a single hat can vary enormously and these days a panama can easily cost anything from a few tens of pounds to more than ten thousand.

Edward VII, unsurprisingly, had one of the costlier ones, which he wore when he went to meet his increasingly bellicose nephew Kaiser Wilhelm II in 1906. Entirely in character, Wilhelm arrived at Cronberg Station to greet his uncle wearing a steel helmet and the pale green full dress uniform of the Posen Chasseurs. Contrastingly, the king chose an altogether

---

* This is still true, although in 2012, handwoven panama hats were added to UNESCO's Intangible Cultural Heritage list.

friendlier hat and an ordinary suit in place of a uniform, which he did in the hope that it would reassure the nervous French that this was a private, family meeting and not a council of war.

In fact His Majesty, whose own father said he took no interest in anything but clothes, was often extravagant in such matters** and is known to have spent around £90 on his French-pleasing hat. This was a staggering sum for a single item of clothing in his day, but perhaps really not that unreasonable for something that will have taken several months to weave and block, all of it by hand and using fibres as thin as the hair of a child. Incredibly, similar hats are still woven this way in Ecuador today, albeit in microscopically small numbers. The best can weigh as little as an ounce but yet have a scarcely believable 4,000 weaves per square inch – and a commensurately high price tag.

Of course, it's perfectly true that a cheaper hat from somewhere other than Ecuador will keep the sun off your head almost as well, but no one's going to mistake its machine-woven fibres for vampire skin, and probably no one will be as transfixed as those Spanish *conquistadors* were 500 years ago.

** On one occasion he sent thirty-four different waistcoats to Savile Row to be cleaned and pressed.

MARINER'S CAP

Perhaps most familiar from grainy black-and-white images of Vladimir Lenin addressing crowds of Russians in 1917, this style of simple, soft-peaked workman's cap was already common in that country and had been worn for at least 100 years before the Bolshevik Revolution.

Lenin's sartorial style was quickly followed by many in his circle. These included Leon Trotsky, Josef Stalin and 'Iron Felix' Dzerzhinsky, the head of both the Cheka and OGPU, the Soviet secret police. Similar hats were also issued to the murderous political commissars, the widely feared state agents charged with maintaining the loyalty and ideological purity of Soviet troops in the Second World War, although even this unsavoury association has done nothing to dent its status as the hat of choice for anyone wishing to advertise his proletarian credentials.

China's communist leader Mao Zedong was often photographed wearing something similar in the early 1950s. A decade later Bob Dylan put one on for his eponymous 1962 debut, all four Beatles wore them while touring the US (years before John Lennon wrote 'Working Class Hero' for the Plastic Ono Band) and these days a blue corduroy version is commonly seen perched on the head of Labour Party MP Jeremy Corbyn.

The original nineteenth-century hats were simple, cheap and practical woollen garments and as such were completely unfreighted by any political symbolism. Blue or black ones were worn by literally millions of working-class men and boys throughout the Russian Empire, not just sailors but also artisans and factory hands, and by fishermen in some Greek coastal communities.

In Russia at least, their status changed in the 1840s when Tsar Nicholas I announced a ban on Jewish men growing their traditional *pe'ot* or long sidelocks. Nearly five million Jews, most of whom were forced to live in a restricted zone called the Pale of Settlement, were also forbidden to wear any traditional Jewish clothing or headgear. The mariner's cap seemed an obvious alternative and a decorated felt version called the *kashket* or *dashiki* quickly became associated with the empire's Jewish population.*

When members of this community managed to escape Tsarist and then Communist persecution by fleeing to the West, their caps frequently went with them. Examples can be seen in numberless photographs of the millions of Jews murdered by the Nazis in Occupied Europe. Others were worn by workers on the collective farms (or *kibbutzim*) which were established by and for Holocaust survivors lucky enough to find their way to Israel.

In the UK the hat has also enjoyed periodic revivals, for example in the 1950s among bikers (in emulation of Marlon Brando's character Johnny Strabler in *The Wild One*) and in the 1960s when 'folkies' such as Donovan followed the lead set by Dylan's idol, Woodie Guthrie. It has remained popular on the water too, although chiefly among leisure sailors and whale watchers rather than professional mariners.

---

* Topol's character Tevye the Dairyman wears one in the vaunted 1964 film adaption of *Fiddler on the Roof*, so they are sometimes known as fiddler's caps.

BRODIE HELMET

The lack of protective headgear in the trenches was just one of many different indicators that no one really had any idea what to expect from the Great War.

As casualty figures began to rise, it didn't take long for the authorities on both sides to acknowledge that something simple and strong was urgently needed to reduce the horrifying number of head injuries. With so many thousands of troops in the field of battle, this meant an industrialised product that could be produced quickly and in quantity. The Munitions Invention Department at the War Office in Pall Mall* was confident that the Imperial Germany Army's comically anachronistic spiked *pickelhaub* was not an idea worth copying. It also rejected the French design of the time (on the grounds that it was 'both too flimsy and too expensive to manufacture') and turned to an inventor called John Leopold Brodie for help.

Born in Riga (as Leopold Janno Braude), Brodie had reportedly made his fortune as an associate of Cecil Rhodes in the South African gold and diamond fields. After settling in London, he falsely claimed to have invented the traffic light,** but he was responsible for several other innovations, including a small rocket designed to carry messages across no man's land and a type of military gas detector.

For this new War Office commission, Brodie experimented with several different designs before settling on a simple bowl shape. With its shallow, domed crown and a wide brim it looked something like a medieval *chapel de fer*, but it had the decided advantage of being exceptionally quick to manufacture. Each helmet could be stamped out in a single pressing from thick,

---

* The site is now occupied by the Royal Automobile Club, which incorporates a few architectural features from the older building.

** At least according to newspaper reports at the time. In fact, London's first traffic lights were erected in Parliament Square in 1868, five years before Brodie was even born. Unfortunately, this early gas-powered contrivance exploded, killing a policeman and causing the horses of a passing cavalry platoon to stampede.

20-gauge sheet metal, which meant it was cheap to produce as well as serviceable and robust.

The shape offered excellent protection from bullets and shrapnel, something Brodie attempted to demonstrate by putting on his prototype and inviting interested parties to fire a .45-calibre bullet at his head. While it is not clear whether or not anyone took him up on this, the War Office was sufficiently impressed to order an initial batch of 1,000 hats with only minor modifications to Brodie's original. These were sent to the front line for evaluation. By the time official approval was granted in July 1916 – just in time for the Battle of the Somme – more than a million of Brodie's helmets were in service.

It has since been claimed that the protection offered by the Brodie was considered less important at the time than the speed and ease with which huge numbers of them could be manufactured, although it is clear that a good deal of thought went into the helmet's construction.

The rival French M15 or 'Adrian' helmet was cheaper and relatively light, but it comprised four major metal components riveted together. Because of this, each helmet reportedly involved seventy different processes to manufacture, which was clearly far too many given the numbers of troops who had to be kitted out. Also, the design was based on an ornamental helmet worn by the Parisian fire brigade and its mild-carbon-steel construction put soldiers at great risk from the high-speed projectiles that had begun to cause so much death and destruction along the Western Front.***

*** Despite these drawbacks, Winston Churchill was an enthusiast. After crossing the Channel to re-join the Queen's Own Oxfordshire Hussars on the Western Front (his pre-war regiment), and characteristically completely against regulations, he put on a French helmet to protect what he called his 'valuable cranium'. According to Lord Jenkins of Hillhead, one of several biographers, the shape 'much suited his martial frown'.

In all, more than 3 million Adrians were produced, some of which found their way into the Italian, Russian, Romanian, Belgian and Serbian armies. The Brodie was far more successful, however, and actually far superior. It was manufactured using mangalloy, a manganese-steel alloy which had been formulated in the 1880s by the distinguished metallurgist Sir Robert Hadfield. By blending steel with 10–15 per cent manganese and only 1 per cent carbon, much higher impact strength could be obtained without adding additional weight.

Weight was a crucial consideration for wearers. While no one could pretend that the 2lb 4oz (1kg) helmet was comfortable, even with the later, improved rubber lining tubes, it was essential that a soldier felt happy enough to keep his on – typically for hours at a time and sometimes for several days.

So-called Hadfield steel offered impressive resistance not just to shrapnel and other flying debris (such as the stones thrown up during heavy artillery bombardments) but to rounds fired directly at the wearer. Tests showed a helmet could withstand a .45-calibre bullet, fired from just 3 metres away and travelling at 180 metres a second. More anecdotal evidence suggests that because of this British helmets were as much as 50 per cent safer than the Adrians worn by other troops. Lower-velocity projectiles were deflected by the Brodie's curved shape, while rubber buffer tubes inside the helmet helped to reduce the blunt trauma that would otherwise have resulted from a powerful impact.

Its manifest qualities notwithstanding, however, the Brodie was not received with unanimous acclaim. In 1917, George V was photographed wearing one in the desolate wasteland of Wytshaete Ridge (during one of his five visits to the trenches), but several senior officers, possibly feeling slighted because they had not been consulted by the War Office, thought the hats looked 'unsoldierly'. There were even suggestions from some of the more traditionally minded among them that issuing this sort of protective headgear would simply make the troops go soft.

A few of the criticisms were more intelligent. Early lining materials were found to be too slippery, which could make a helmet unbalanced. (This was hastily rectified.) There were also sensible concerns that the sun reflecting off a steel helmet risked giving away a concealed soldier's position. On the German side the problem was tackled by covering helmets with grey cloth, as one officer put it 'so that the ornaments would not glitter in the sun'. For British troops the issue was successfully addressed by texturing the surface using paint mixed with sand or sawdust, or by covering the helmet with camouflaged material.

In general, though, Brodie's creation must be viewed as a resounding success, a genuine triumph of form through function. 'Cases have occurred in which the wearers have been hit but saved by these helmets from what without them would have meant certain death,' reported the *Illustrated London News*. 'Even in cases of extreme risk, not only has death been avoided, but injuries have been confined to bruises or superficial wounds.'

Little wonder then that the design was so widely adopted. British and Empire troops of all ranks were issued with them (under the official designation 'Helmet, Steel, Mark I') and before long the United States Quartermaster General had also taken an interest. Initially the Americans placed an order for 400,000 British-made helmets, but then in 1918 they began manufacturing their own version called the M1917. Brodie himself later upped sticks and relocated across the Atlantic.

By the war's end, somewhere between 7.5 and 9 million of his helmets had been manufactured in literally dozens of different factories and workshops around the world. The Mk I remained in service in Britain all the way through to 1940,*

---

* That year a new, slightly modified Mk II version was introduced. This was issued to all three branches of HM Forces as well as to Air Raid Precaution (ARP) wardens, the police and fire brigade, and was still in service in 1945. A cheaper version, costing just 5s 6d (27½p), was produced for volunteer firewatchers.

although even this long service has not prevented it being thought of primarily as an icon of the Great War and in particular the Western Front.

Indeed, because it was one of the first pieces of equipment designed specifically for conditions along the Franco-Belgian frontier, it seems fitting that one of the most moving pieces of trench art in the Historial de la Grande Guerre in France (The Museum of the Great War) isn't just another engraved shell case or a crossed pair of rifle rounds but a genuine Brodie. This one is very particular and has a painting on it showing the nearby battle-shattered town hall at Péronne. It is not known who painted it, but as British troops occupied the town in early 1917, it seems reasonable to suppose it was the work of its original owner, an ordinary Tommy.

HARD HAT

The traditional yellow protective hard hat worn by construction workers was invented by the novelist and short story writer Franz Kafka in 1912. Apparently he came up with the idea while processing injury compensation claims for the Worker's Accident Insurance Institute in Prague. That's the claim anyway (and Kafka *was* an insurance lawyer) but sadly no documentation has ever been found to prove it.

Far more likely is that the first proper lightweight hard hats were produced by the mining-equipment company E.D. Bullard. In 1919 it began selling something based on the steel Brodie Helmet (p.187) which had saved so many Allied soldiers' lives during the Great War.

Protective helmets of a sort certainly existed prior to this. English shipwrights are known to have dipped their own hats into pitch or tar before drying them out in the sun, and E.D. Bullard itself had already produced a limited range of leather helmets for the gold- and copper-mining industries.

Staff at the company recognised that military helmets were far more effective – the founder's son, Edward Bullard, had survived a spell as a young cavalry officer on the Western Front – but they were also too heavy for civilian use. The lieutenant's answer was something he called the Hard Boiled Hat. This recreated the basic shape of his old Brodie using steamed or boiled canvas, leather, glue and a black shellac finish. The latter is a hardened paste made from the resin secreted by the female Asian lac bug, *Kerria lacca*. Between 1930 and the war years it was the main component of phonograph discs or 78s.

The result was a light but strong shape and one which could be produced at relatively low cost. The company later incorporated suspension bands inside the hat. These helped to spread the weight of it, as well as to reduce the force on the wearer's hat of any accidental blow or impact. The US Navy was one of the first customers, along with Six Companies Inc. (builders of the giant Hoover Dam) and San Francisco's new Golden Gate

Bridge. The latter was the first construction site anywhere in the world which compelled workers to wear hard hats, and when the bridge was completed in 1937 it was without a single death or serious injury from falling objects.

Over time the only real change to the design has been the choice of material. Boiled canvas quickly gave way to aluminium, aluminium to Bakelite,* Bakelite to fibreglass and finally fibreglass to thermoplastics such as polyethylene or polycarbonate resin. The latter are easy to mould and shape and can be self-coloured to indicate the wearer's role on site: yellow for labourers, blue for electrical workers, white for supervisors and so on.

That the hats play an important role is beyond doubt, although it can sometimes seem as though most of them are worn by politicians and news reporters visiting factories for one photo op or another. Literally billions of pounds are spent on new ones each year, and around the world millions of people wear them every working day. No one can say quite how many lives have been saved in this way, although there is plenty of evidence in Britain and abroad showing that many of those killed or seriously affected by head injuries in hard-hat areas didn't have one on at the time. That's got to say something.

---

* Bakelite or polyoxybenzylmethylenglycolanhydride was invented by the Belgian chemist Leo Baekeland in 1907.

CLOCHE HAT

The definitive headgear of the 1920s flapper and London's Bright Young Things,* the unstructured felt cloche was the most fashionable refinement of the bell-like hats which first appeared in Britain during the Edwardian Period.

Its invention is usually attributed to Caroline Reboux (1837–1927), the self-styled 'Queen of the Milliners' in pre-war Paris, although a rival claim is sometimes made for Lucy Hamar who began selling something similar around the same time.

Reboux remains a somewhat mysterious character. She contrived for herself a colourful backstory, claiming to be the orphaned daughter of an impoverished aristocrat, but was enormously successful and a considerable innovator once she began working on her own account. During a long career she routinely employed as many as 150 women in several workshops supplying her own shops in Paris and London as well as others she helped launch in Chicago and New York.

Reboux was well connected, good friends with Jean Cocteau as well as the left-wing statesman Leon Blum, and her early clients included Marlene Dietrich, Princess Metternich and the last Empress of the French, Napoleon III's widow Eugénie. Wallis Simpson wore a Reboux hat when she married the former Edward VIII in 1937, and although the company eventually collapsed in the 1950s, several hundred of its creations are preserved at the Musée de la Mode et du Textile in the French capital.

Reboux was known for her clean, simple style and always preferred fabrics to be draped and cut with a minimum of extraneous details. Even if the idea for the cloche came from someone else, there seems little doubt that it was she and her high-profile patrons who did the most to popularise the now almost epoch-defining design. For many wearers, its stripped-back,

---

* It's the first thing the narrator of Michael Arlen's *The Green Hat* (1924) notices about the book's glamorous but ultimately tragic, Hispano-Suiza-driving heroine.

minimalist style represented a welcome break with the extravagant bonnets of the pre-war period. Throughout the Roaring Twenties, there appeared to be no better accompaniment to the clean, straight-cut flapper style with its preference for androgynous haircuts, flat chests, kohl-rimmed eyes and elaborate, angular Art Deco jewellery.

Looking back, it's easy to overstate the feminist argument, but what the French made, British women bought in great numbers. The 'Brideshead Set' is not remembered for its alignment with the suffragette cause, but to many of its members the cloche seemed genuinely liberating and it quickly became an essential element of a new look that promised to free wearers from fusty, pre-war ideas about femininity.

Worn snug against the head, the cloche went perfectly with newly fashionable, shorter and low-maintenance hairstyles such as the shingle-bob and Eton crop. Also, because it was pulled down low across the eyes, wearers were forced to hold their heads slightly higher than usual, thereby conveying an attractive (if slightly haughty) air of self-confidence and self-sufficiency.

This aspect of the design now looks critical to its success. The deaths of so many young men in the trenches (and of millions more in the Spanish flu epidemic which followed) had encouraged many privileged young women to think more about their lives and their independence. In increasing numbers they seemed determined to enjoy their twenties rather than sitting at home waiting for a decent chap to propose after a game of tennis. To a generation of women who had taken to smoking and drinking in public, listening to jazz, experimenting with sex and even learning to drive motor cars, the cloche represented something fresh and new and very different. It chimed perfectly with its buyers' shifting expectations.

The basic cloche design also turned out to be impressively versatile, despite its apparent simplicity. Thousands were made without decoration, but they could just as easily be embellished with a luxuriant spray of flowers or feathers, or worn with a piece of jewellery pinned to the side. The felt could be embroidered or carry appliqué decorations, or indeed be replaced by straw or sisal for the summer months. Once more elaborate jewelled and beaded cloches began appearing at evening events (and even on the heads of brides), the style can be said to have well and truly arrived.

In 1925, Coco Chanel, no mean milliner herself, was photographed in a cloche at the Grand National with her lover Bendor, 2nd Duke of Westminster. And when Greta Garbo wore a cloche in her first 'talkie' – an adaptation of Eugene O'Neill's *Anna Christie* – sales went through the roof.* Anxious not to miss out on this rising trend, leading couturiers such as Britain's Edward Molyneux and Jeanne-Marie Lanvin began opening their own ateliers to manufacture hats that precisely matched their clothes instead of just buying them in.

Reboux, however, was unusually adept at staying one step ahead of the competition. It was she who first thought of adding a veil to a hat. By 'swathing the feminine face in a mist' (as one admirer put it), she managed to create yet another millinery sensation, although her death at 90 robbed her of the chance to see the example worn to such great effect in the 1932 film *Shanghai Express* by her old patron Marlene Dietrich.

Dietrich's moody ensemble was the work of Munich-born Hans Harberger, a leading society and cinematic milliner who liked to be known as 'Mr John'. He went on to dress Vivien Leigh in *Gone With the Wind*, Garbo in *The Painted Veil* and Marilyn Monroe in *Gentlemen Prefer Blondes*, but fell foul of Gypsy Rose Lee after showing the American entertainer his new collection in the mid 50s.

---

* 'Garbo Talks!' screamed the posters, and her opening line was eminently quotable: 'Give me a whisky, ginger ale on the side. And don't be stingy, baby.'

Lee bought one of the new hats** and made a dozen copies which she gave to friends as Easter presents. Harberger was furious and rang to protest. 'Darling,' said Lee, 'I'm so glad you called. I made a few copies of your marvellous hat, and I need some labels. The hats look so naked without them.' The milliner agreed to send some, but when these arrived they read 'A MR JOHN DESIGN STOLEN BY GYPSY ROSE LEE'. Eventually he shut up shop after complaining that women no longer had any real sense of style and now preferred what he described as 'orthopaedic hairdos and french-fried curls'.

The cloche managed to outlive its likely creator, but not by much. By 1933 the craze was all but over. It's made the odd, brief reappearance since then, but its ubiquity during the inter-war period means it is now almost impossible to believe that it was once, quite genuinely, revolutionary.

** At least she paid for it. Once, on leaving a drinks party in Cambridge, the author H.G. Wells picked up his host's hat by mistake and went home. Realising what he'd done he decided not to return it, and wrote to the owner saying: 'I stole your hat, I like your hat. I shall keep your hat. Whenever I look inside it I shall think of you and your excellent sherry and of the town of Cambridge. I take off your hat to you.'

HOMBURG

The original of this was a type of nineteenth-century stiffened-felt German hunting hat but the homburg's story really belongs to the 1930s. It was then that it became so closely associated with one British politician, the Foreign Secretary of the day, that it is still sometimes known as an Anthony Eden, or just an Eden, in Savile Row.

The hat had first appeared in Britain in August 1882 when the Prince of Wales wore one on his return from a trip to a German spa town, Bad Homburg, where the English upper classes liked to go to take the cure.* The style suited him, and British visitors to the spa started buying similar hats made at the town's Möckel factory. According to his biographers, the prince found this deeply flattering, which was encouragement enough for still more of his mother's subjects to follow his lead.

In 1923's *The Inimitable Jeeves,* Bertie Wooster tells his valet, 'Then bring me my whangee [cane], my yellowest shoes, and the old green Homburg' – but by this time the factory was in trouble. It closed in 1931, although homburgs remained highly fashionable and Eden's – usually a black felt one with a silk brim – was by no means the only homburg to adorn the head of a senior parliamentarian. Prime Minister Neville Chamberlain was another wearer; so too, inevitably, was his eventual successor at No. 10, Winston Churchill.

When an effigy of the former was burned at a Sussex bonfire night celebration in 1938 (feelings were running higher than normal after an official in Whitehall instructed the England football team to give a Nazi salute before a match in Berlin), Harold Macmillan, then still a backbencher, cheerfully donated one of his own black homburgs and a rolled up umbrella to give it the authentic touch.

---

* The rich also went there to gamble. This was illegal in Britain at the time and Gladstone was appalled to read about the Prince 'gambling away the gold that had been wrung from the toil and sweat of the working man'.

Unlike Chamberlain, though, Eden was a popular figure (at least until his resignation after the Suez debacle) and his personal style was definitely part of his appeal. As an exceptionally young Foreign Secretary (he was only 38) he cut a dash in the Commons, especially when seen alongside colleagues who were typically much older. Perhaps because of this, no one batted an eyelid when later, having married Churchill's niece, he moved into Beau Brummel's old townhouse at 4 Chesterfield Street in Mayfair. It all seemed perfectly appropriate.

In the US, *Time* magazine referred in a glowing editorial to his 'pin-stripe trousers, modish short jacket and swank black felt hat' after one of his trips abroad, and when Eden visited New York he was inundated by hundreds of pieces of fan mail from women of all ages. Observers closer to home were if anything even more complimentary. The writer Robert Graves likened his moustache to that of the Hollywood star Clark Gable; more than once he has been described as the best-looking prime minister of either sex of the twentieth century; and a decade after his death in 1977, Alan Clarke MP still recalled the luxurious scent of his expensive cologne.

Not for nothing were Eden and his acolytes known as the 'glamour boys'. Even left-wing opponents such as the journalist Malcolm Muggeridge conceded that he was handsome, and when some of his political manoeuvring looked weak and indecisive another Harold (Nicolson) was still able to acknowledge that, although Eden got things wrong, he did so with an 'exquisite elegance'. Admittedly one Scots earl found him as 'vain as a peacock with all the mannerisms of a *petit maître*' (meaning a fop) and Eden is known to have varnished his fingernails. But the peer in question was getting on a bit by then, and everyone knew him to be a terrible old snob.

For his part, the diarist and socialite MP Sir Henry 'Chips' Channon was convinced that, Eden or no Eden, once Chamberlain began falling out of favour over his appeasement of Hitler so did the homburg. 'Everyone wears bowlers now,' he wrote in his diary for June 1938, 'black homburgs are out.'

But this was far from true: Eden carried on with his and Churchill was still wearing a homburg after the war. So were Hercule Poirot, Tony Hancock and Konrad Adenauer, the new German Chancellor, and across the Atlantic Dwight D. Eisenhower wore them at both of his presidential inaugurations in 1953 and 1957. The second of these even acquired a name – the 'international' – because it had taken craftsmen from at least ten different countries so long to make.* Similar craftsmen still make homburgs today, although they are now only rarely worn.

---

* Al Pacino's character Michael Corleone also wears a homburg in *The Godfather*, which spans a similar period.

IMPERIAL STATE CROWN

Although the present state crown was made only recently, by Garrard & Co. in 1937 for George VI, it has existed in some form since at least Henry V's reign (1413–22). It is traditionally worn after, but not during, the actual coronation at Westminster Abbey, and at formal occasions such as the State Opening of Parliament.

By any standards it is a breathtaking object. Henry's crown was probably fairly simple but many of his successors proved unable to resist adding their own embellishments. These included great numbers of precious stones as well as miniatures of Jesus Christ, the Virgin Mary and St George, and by the time of Elizabeth I it must have been a magnificent sight, as it was set with 168 pearls, fifty-eight rubies, twenty-eight diamonds, nineteen sapphires and two large emeralds. It is thought to have weighed around 3.3kg before it was broken up on Cromwell's orders and sold off with the rest of the royal regalia for £1,100.

This shameful act of vandalism was impossible to reverse. One eleventh-century crown belonging to Edith of Wessex fetched a paltry £16 and only a few precious components have ever been recovered. These are Queen Elizabeth's pearl earrings, a sapphire that had been buried with Edward the Confessor (Edith's husband) in 1066 and the Black Prince ruby worn by Henry V at Agincourt and by Richard III at Bosworth Field.*

Only a 1,000-year-old spoon and a sacred gold ampulla somehow escaped the looters, presumably because no one realised the important part they played in the coronation ceremony. As a result Charles II was forced to commission entirely new regalia at the start of his reign and when he did so he asked for the recovered jewels to be incorporated into his new Crown of State.

---

* A crown containing the ruby, actually a 170-carat cabochon balas or spinel, was allegedly retrieved from a hawthorn bush after Richard had been killed. It was later used by the Earl of Richmond to declare himself Henry VII, the first of the Tudor kings.

Happily the same stones are still present in the Imperial State Crown, together with the famous cushion-shaped Cullinan II. Otherwise known as the Second Star of Africa, this is the second largest stone cut from the mighty Cullinan Diamond, the largest diamond ever discovered.

This mammoth find, fully 4 inches long, was made on a South African farm in 1905. It weighed 3,025 carats, or more than half a kilogramme, when it was presented, uncut, to King Edward VII on his birthday. The extraordinary gift was intended as a symbolic gesture to heal the rift between Britain and South Africa after the Boer War. It was probably impossible to value accurately even then, but at a time when English farm-workers typically earned less than a pound a week, the farm owner received £150,000 compensation.**

The king had the stone cut by Joseph Asscher of Amsterdam, who studied the huge stone every day for three months before raising his cleaver's blade. At the first blow the steel blade broke, at the second Asscher is said to have fainted. Eventually he went on to produce nine large stones from the monster and nearly 100 smaller ones. Several unpolished fragments were also left when the largest stone, Cullinan I (the Star of Africa), was mounted in the Sovereign's Sceptre. Cullinan II was placed in the front of the band of the Imperial State Crown, and the remaining stones were made into jewellery but do not form part of the official Crown Jewels.

In all the Imperial State Crown contains 2,868 diamonds in silver mounts and seventeen sapphires, eleven emeralds, five mixed-cut rubies and 269 pearls in gold ones. The whole ensemble weighs just over one kilogramme. This is less than half the weight of the much older St Edward's Crown, which is used for the actual coronation.

** The Crown Jewels as a whole are now estimated to be worth between £3–5 billion, although one wonders how such a figure is calculated.

Even so, the Queen has admitted that, at the State Opening of Parliament, 'you can't look down to read the speech, you have to take the speech up,' and in October 2019, for the first time, the crown was placed on a cushion next to the throne, and Her Majesty instead wore the lighter George IV diadem.

For her own coronation in 1953 the crown was shortened by an inch. This was done by Garrard, the Crown Jewellers, but Lock & Co. in St James's devised a special fitment to make it more comfortable. On seeing it for the first time, the Duke of Edinburgh is supposed to have asked: 'Where did you get that hat?' This was a reference to a humorous song written by Joseph J. Sullivan, an American acrobat and music hall comedian:

Where did you get that hat?
Where did you get that hat?
Isn't it a nobby one
And just the proper style?

Her Majesty's response is not known.

BERET

Berets have been around for generations, and something similar is known to have been worn by Bronze Age Minoans and Villanovan Etruscans, but in Britain the date to remember is 5 March 1924. That's the day the sartorially fastidious and deeply conservative-minded George V granted permission for the beret to become standard issue for the men of the Royal Tank Corps, of which he was Colonel-in-Chief.

Ahead of this, a number of different officers seem to have suggested that berets would be the most appropriate headgear for clambering in and out of a tank's small hatch. One of them, Eric 'Chink' Dorman-Smith MC and Bar, became enthused after acquiring a black beret during a tour of Spain's Basque region in the early 1920s with his friend Ernest Hemingway.

Hemingway later wrote a poem in his honour ('To Chink Whose Trade is Soldiering'), and having scored an unprecedented 1,000 out of a 1,000 in the Staff College entrance examination, Dorman-Smith certainly sounds like the kind of talented young officer whose opinions would have carried some weight.

However, although his biographer describes 'a Basque beret from Pamplona' hanging on his wall, it seems just as likely that Chink, like many others serving on the Western Front, would already have seen Frenchmen wearing berets in and out of the trenches. Infantrymen of the 70th Chasseurs Alpins had already been wearing them since the days of the Third Republic.* In 1918 they trained with the Royal Tank Corps (RTC) and most British tank commanders would have quickly grasped the suitability of their hats as an alternative to the conventional peaked cap which made it so awkward to see properly through a tank's narrow, letterbox-like apertures. A beret would avoid this problem but still give a man's head a degree of protection from

---

* Their berets have had a hunting horn insignia since 1889 which isn't jaune (yellow) but jonquille (daffodil) in line with the regiment's idiosyncratic tradition of avoiding using the names of certain colours.

grease and knocks. It could also be stowed away in a tank's cramped interior.

Part of the delay in securing permission for the RTC to adopt the new headgear was due to a disagreement over the appropriate style. Major-General Sir Hugh Elles, Inspector of Tank Corps at the War Office, thought the Chasseur beret too sloppy, and the Basque-style *txapela* too skimpy. George V was a notorious stickler for old-fashioned customs and dress, civilian as well as military, and a compromise based on the Scottish tam o'shanter (p.55) had to be devised before Sir Hugh was prepared to seek official approval from the king in November 1923.

Sir Hugh particularly favoured a black beret, as this wouldn't show grease stains, and the idea received royal assent a few months later. For several years the RTC, with its motto 'Fear Naught', had a monopoly on the beret, but in 1939 it was renamed the Royal Tank Regiment and shortly afterwards permission was given to the rest of the Royal Armoured Corps to wear berets of their own.

Before long the Parachute Regiment followed suit, adopting its now famous maroon beret. Green berets began to be worn by Commando units, and khaki berets were issued to members of the Reconnaissance Corps. After blue-grey berets were ordered by the Royal Air Force Regiment, they rapidly began to replace the unpopular General Service Cap as they were issued to all ranks in most regiments of the British Army.

Berets also crossed the line into the civilian sphere around this time, perhaps because hats gave those who wanted it a means of expressing themselves at a time when wartime rationing was causing something of a fashion famine. Others preferred home-made turbans, however, which were often worn by women in munitions factories to protect their hair, or headscarves decorated with a borrowed regimental badge.

Today men and women in almost every British military unit wear berets and different colours are still used to differentiate one unit from another.* The only exceptions to this are the Royal Irish Regiment, which has a beret-*like* hat called the caubeen (an eighteenth-century word meaning 'old hat'), and the tam o'shanters of the Royal Regiment of Scotland.

Despite this ubiquity, however, not to mention the tens of thousands of robin-egg blue ones used to identify United Nations peacekeepers, the world's most famous beret has long been the black woollen one worn by guerrilla leader Che Guevara in his (for once genuinely) iconic 1960 portrait by Alberto Korda.

Entitled *Guerrillero Heroico*, and reproduced literally millions of times on posters, T-shirts, mugs, tea towels and even tattoos, Korda's photograph is one of the most famous of all time. As familiar as NASA's *Earthrise*, the bewitching image of our world captured by Apollo 8 astronaut William Anders as he orbited the Moon on Christmas Eve 1968, it has become a global symbol of youthful idealism, student unrest, counter-culture politics and undefined rebellion.

Even for the young, however, the Marxist revolutionary was always a deeply flawed hero. A callous, cold-hearted executioner, the grim realities of his life sit uneasily with his reputation as the Swinging Sixties' red Robin Hood. It's also highly doubtful that he would have had much enthusiasm for the era of peace and free love that was sweeping the West while he organised his firing squads and one-sided revolutionary tribunals.

Yet somehow none of this seems to matter. Staring into the distance, Korda's subject still mesmerises the onlooker.

---

* The Royal Tank Regiment eventually reasserted its monopoly on black berets, although Field Marshal Montgomery retained his despite being an infantryman. Montgomery claimed it had been given to him by 'the NCO in command of my tank during the Battle of Alamein' and he wore it with two badges instead of one. In 1945 he donated this trademark garment to the Tank Museum at Bovington Camp in Dorset.

Brooding, intense, somehow at once Christ-like *and* sexy, it's not just his face that gives the picture its power but also his beret. Austerely sober, unadorned except for its small red star, it says 'this is a man of action'. Never mind his hippie hair. Never mind the unshaven chin and the straggly moustache. Che's emphatically unmilitary appearance tells you he means business – and Korda's Leica M2 captured that perfectly.

PORK PIE

Another relation of the fedora and the trilby, this emerged as a hat for women in nineteenth-century America and swapped genders at the turn of the century. Its popularity on both sides of the Atlantic received a somewhat surprising boost at the hands of Buster Keaton. In the 1920s the silent movie star picked one as an alternative to the derby favoured by Harold Lloyd and other screen comedy rivals.

Lloyd eventually switched to a straw hat, but Keaton felt his own kind of physical comedy demanded something more robust. He decided to make his own and later explained the process in some detail:

> I took a good Stetson and cut it down, then I stiffened the brim with sugar water. My recipe calls for three heaping tea-spoons of granulated sugar in a teacup of warm water. You wet the top and bottom of the brim, and then smooth it out on a clean, hard surface and let it dry to a good stiffness.

Keaton did a lot of what he called 'water stunts' in his films, and confounding his hopes, the mortality rate was still high, with as many as half a dozen hats destroyed in each film he made. Because of this, he and his wife are estimated to have produced at least a thousand of these conversions over several years, a fair few of which were snatched off the actor's head by boisterous souvenir hunters when he appeared in public.

Eventually people started buying the hats instead of pinch-ing them. With its flat or telescopic crown and short flat brim, the style seems to have exercised a particular hold over zoot-suited jazz and blues musicians after the war. One of the first, American saxophonist Lester Young, reportedly looked so cool in his that when Charles Mingus composed an elegy to him in B-flat, in 1959, he called it 'Goodbye Pork Pie Hat'.

Joni Mitchell in turn added lyrics to the track on her album, *Mingus*, which was released twenty years later.*

Until the 1960s, the hats were far more popular in the USA than in Britain. However, after being adopted almost as a house style by participants in Jamaican 'rude boy' street culture, the fashion for tight mohair suits, narrow ties and pork pie hats followed their music to London. It was picked up by a variety of British ska bands, mods and even skinheads, but then dropped following the reggae invasion, only to be rekindled in the late 1970s as part of a ska revival.

Many of these bands driving the revival, including the Selecter, the Beat and Madness, first appeared on the Two-Tone label. The company was founded by Jerry Dammers of The Specials and was highly influential although short-lived. Its logo included a character called 'Walt Jabsco'. He took his name from an old American bowling shirt owned by Dammers but was sharply dressed in a black suit, black tie, white shirt and white socks – and a pork pie hat.

---

* Mingus died before it was released, but he and his wife both collaborated with Mitchell on this.

RACING HELMET

Karl Benz's invention of the automobile posed as many new problems as it seemed to solve, probably the least of which was what pioneering motorists – or 'motorious carbarians' as *The Times** preferred to call them – ought to wear.

In those early days, before Henry Ford really put the world on wheels with his brilliant Model T, the car was little more than a rich man's plaything and many bizarre outfits were trialled by the few who could afford it. The most outlandish of these included a sort of cape-cum-tent called the Avalon Storm Apron. This was designed to envelop four or five occupants at a time and had separate openings cut into the rubberised cloth so the driver and passengers could all poke their heads out to see (and to breathe).

Simpler kid-lined leather masks and a variety of 'dust-proof motor veils' were offered to female automobilists, while Dunhill's Conduit Street showroom advertised what it called Bobby Finders in several of the better magazines and newspapers. Worn beneath a peaked cap, these were goggles which incorporated magnifying binoculars, thereby enabling drivers to 'spot a policeman at half a mile even if disguised as a respectable man'.

Once cars were fast enough to be raced with conviction, however, the concern needed to shift from comfort and weather protection to personal safety. As early as 1914, the Auto Cycle Union had made so-called skid lids compulsory for anyone racing on two wheels but there were no official regulations relating to racing cars. Throughout the 1920s and '30s grand prix drivers were still wearing pretty much what they liked, which was fine as long as nothing went wrong.

The many photographs showing the most talented of them giving his raised right-arm salute to Adolf Hitler are damning:

---

* In 1896, after Walter Arnold was fined by a court in Tunbridge Wells for driving at more than 2mph, the newspaper became a strong opponent to government plans to raise the speed limit to 14mph.

Rudolf Caracciola was, wretchedly, an enthusiastic member of a Nazi Party paramilitary organisation. He nevertheless looked genuinely dashing when he was racing, his peaked cap turned backwards (in the manner of the earliest aviators) as he wrestled with the wheel of a monstrous, bellowing Mercedes-Benz SS.

Many of the German's less successful rivals favoured soft flying helmets instead, but whether these were made of cloth or fine chamois leather, they can't have offered much more protection than Caracciola hoped to get from his woven-wool. Others, including the 5th Earl Howe, Goldie Gardner and Sammy Davies in Britain, opted for 'corkers' made by Everitt W. Vero & Company in London – which were slightly better, although not by much.

This family-owned firm had been in business since the 1890s making sola topees and then flying helmets for the Royal Flying Corps. The design of its first corker was based on the Calcutta polo helmet, itself an adaptation of the sola topee with a truncated brim. Under the company's 'Everoak' brand, these gradually acquired some useful refinements as the complexities and implications of brain injuries became better understood, including temple protectors, cotton-web concussion tapes and shock-absorbing cork padding.

Much of the information about this sort of thing came from Professor Sir Hugh Cairns, a neurosurgeon who had tried to save his friend T.E. Lawrence ('of Arabia') after the latter's disastrous crash on his Brough Superior motorbike in May 1935. Sir Hugh's efforts were not successful – Lawrence died a few days later – but his findings helped to promote the wider use of helmets for motorcyclists, civilian and military, although it wasn't until 1954 that a proper, modern hard-shell helmet finally appeared, meaning one specifically designed and manufactured for motor racing.

The first of these was manufactured by Roy Richter, the owner of Bell Auto Parts in California, who'd lost a close friend to a racing accident. His Bell 500 was the result of many years' research, much of it by former Navy pilot Frank Heacox, who helped Richter reverse-engineer various different helmets including the latest military ones.

The Bell 500 was impressive and had a polyurethane foam liner inside a hand-laminated fibreglass shell. Laminating by hand was costly, but Richter firmly believed it made the helmet stronger. His theory was shortly put to the test by a team contesting the 1954 Mexican Carrera Panamericana – widely considered to be the most dangerous motor race of the era, it was scrapped after seven people were killed during the event – and then again by Cal Niday, a one-legged former hairdresser who was competing in the Indianapolis 500.*

Unfortunately Niday crashed badly on lap 177 and suffered multiple major injuries, including a fractured skull. He recovered, however, and continued driving, and happily credited the helmet with saving his life. By the following year sales of Richter's helmets were running so far ahead of expectations that he decided to launch a second business dedicated solely to producing more helmets like the Bell 500.

Sales of these took another leap forward when Evel Knievel provided Richter with a similar endorsement to Niday's. The young motorcycle daredevil had come down hard after failing to leap the fountain at Caesars Palace in Las Vegas. The impact smashed his pelvis, and broke a wrist and both ankles – but Knievel's head was fine, although as a result of his high-profile stunts he was reported to have been turned down for life insurance by Lloyds of London no fewer than thirty-seven times.

Even without celebrity testimonials of this sort, though, the efficacy of modern helmets has never been in any serious doubt. Formula One will never be anything other than highly

---

* Unbelievably, he is one of a trio of one-legged drivers who have competed in the famous race. The other two are his near-contemporary Bill Schindler and Al Miller who raced at the 'Brickyard' in the 1930s.

dangerous, but the number of fatalities is far lower now than in any previous decade and only a very small proportion of deaths are the result of injuries to the head and neck.

Bell and Bell-style helmets have also become one of the most colourful and most collectible pieces of racing memorabilia, and at the time of writing the record price paid for one of them at auction is an astonishing £142,000. The helmet in question was worn by Ayrton Senna during the 1990 season. The previous record of £74,750 was achieved by the same driver's 1991 helmet at an earlier auction.

CASQUETTE

Hats and cycling have a long history together. The first bicyclist to win a race, James Moore in 1868, wore a jacket and plus-fours and something a bit like a bowler. Other cyclists wore pill-boxes with chinstraps, or simple tweed caps, but by the 1950s and '60s the colourful little cotton *casquette* had edged these out to become ubiquitous in professional road-racing circles. Examples of the style can be seen in almost all of the most iconic images of the era's greats, including Merckx, Gimondi, Lebaube and De Vlaeminck.

Until the 1990s, the cap's simple design helped keep Tour de France riders cool in summer* and provided at least a degree of warmth in winter. For a while Tour leaders wore yellow caps, their peaks often flipped up like a jockey's or down to protect the rider's eyes from both the sun and rain. Turned around backwards, these offered a slight improvement to a rider's aerodynamic profile as well as shielding vulnerable necks from the otherwise inevitable sunburn.

Race caps were also useful for carrying a sponsor's branding as money flowed into the sport, or at least they were until the introduction of cycle helmets. These quickly became mandatory for competition riders, although *casquettes* are still sometimes worn by competitors under their helmets and by many of the spectators. Riders also routinely put them on to be photographed on the winners' podium, although there is now something delightfully old fashioned about the style, as there is with the little motorised dernys used to set the pace in Japanese *Keirin* races.

In the USA, an estimated two-thirds of all cyclists admitted to hospital had head injuries, so the switch to helmets was long overdue and bound to happen. Even so, many of the riders refused to race in 1991 when the Union Cycliste Internationale

---

* Some riders soaked theirs in iced water before a race. Others were rumoured to grab a cabbage or lettuce leaf from the fridge and slot it in underneath.

first proposed introducing protective headgear. The ruling body persisted, however, and helmets were finally made compulsory in 2003 after the death of a 29-year-old competitor from Kazakhstan.

Other sports have had to make similar transitions, of course, including cricket, where caps have been replaced by helmets with grilles or visors to protect the face, and at most equestrian events. Often these are made of carbon fibre or Kevlar, the sort of expensive and exotic materials borrowed from Formula One cars. Competitors in international dressage still wear short top hats but in the equally traditional arena of the Guards Polo Club, the Duke of Edinburgh, as its founding president, has done much to encourage the wearing of hard-shell helmets on – a style still known as the HRH Pattern.

PILLBOX HAT

It's easy enough to draw a line from the Roman *pileus pannonicus* to the modern pillbox (with or without its veil) and similar hats were certainly being designed and sold by Parisian milliners between the wars. However, this military-style fashion accessory really belongs to the late 1950s and 1960s, and the fashion for them received a major boost in Britain and in the USA when Jackie Kennedy put on a beige one (or 'bone wool' as the *Encyclopaedia of Fashion* called it) for her husband's 1961 inauguration.

JFK was never a great fan of hats, and neither was his First Lady. It is even claimed that the American hat-making industry was fatally damaged by the president's refusal to wear its products* and that sales of men's hats began to decline as soon as he turned up, hatless, for his swearing-in.

Actually this can't be true: it was his successor Lyndon B. Johnson who refused to wear a top hat for any part of his own inauguration in 1965, and all subsequent presidents have followed suit. JFK actually did wear the traditional silk top and wore it for most of the day. He only took it off to address the crowd and thereafter, as the 35th President of the United States, he often carried a hat and was careful to ensure that its maker's label was always visible to any photographers likely to show an interest.

It is true, however, that sales of men's hats were falling off a cliff at this time, but JFK can hardly be blamed for failing to halt the slide. We've already heard how his predecessor Eisenhower preferred a homburg to a top hat, but he was frequently photographed without any hat at all, and the era of greater informality was beginning to creep in years before Kennedy made it into the Oval Office.

---

* Closer to home, a similar accusation has been levelled at the Duke of Edinburgh, although his decision to wear a bowler hat during a visit to the 1949 London Ideal Home Exhibition was said at the time to have done much to improve sales.

In the USA, 1951 was a particularly poor year for sales, perhaps because many of Kennedy's generation had tired of wearing helmets, hats and caps of all styles with their uniforms during the war years. In Britain hats for women were still de rigeur on smart occasions, so were long gloves, but then things changed when Mary Quant declared that she didn't want to grow up because 'it meant having candy-floss hair, stiletto heels, girdles and great boobs'. Suddenly many younger people, already becoming non-conformist and increasingly casual, found they didn't really care one way or the other what anyone in authority chose to wear.

It has also been suggested that the design of newer, more streamlined motor cars made it impractical to wear a hat. In the 1920s the aforementioned 5th Earl of Lonsdale replaced the body of his Rolls-Royce 20hp with one from a (taller) Daimler so he could keep his hat on, but these days only London's black taxis are designed with sufficient headroom for a large hat. Even this, however, doesn't explain why millions of commuters stopped wearing anything at all on their heads when so many of them travelled to work not in cars at all but by train.**

The First Lady sensibly owned a James Lock 'Quorn' for riding but as a rule she disliked hats as much as JFK did. She was nevertheless fully aware that protocol required her to wear something suitable for her husband's inauguration. Dior and Givenchy both had pillboxes in their collections by this time and Mrs Kennedy was an elegant, confirmed Francophile. However, she realised that something homegrown was called

---

** One of Britain's biggest carmakers, William Morris of Morris Motors, remained a habitual hat wearer. Eventually ennobled as Viscount Nuffield, this country's greatest-ever philanthropist established a new college at Oxford. Before doing so, he was invited to dine at Magdalen and afterwards called at the porter's lodge to collect his hat. Astonished at the speed with which this was produced, he asked how the porter knew it was his. The porter replied, 'I don't, My Lord, but it's the one you came with.'

for on such an important public occasion and so turned to an up-and-coming young American designer called Roy Halston Frowick for help.

At the time Halston, as he wished to be known, was employed as head milliner at the Bergdorf Goodman store on New York's Fifth Avenue. His designs were known for their chic simple minimalism. His modest little pillbox was a hat Mrs Kennedy was happy to wear, and one she could see would be the perfect accompaniment for the clean-cut Oleg Cassini suit she was planning to wear.

Cassini's real name was Oleg Aleksandrovich Loiewski. He was born in France in 1913 but went on to serve with the US military during the Second World War, acquiring impeccable American credentials along the way, which belied his name and Russian/Italian ancestry. Together with Halston, he created what became known as the 'Jackie Look', and was soon nicknamed the Secretary of Style in White House circles.

Cassini's style, like Halston's, was quiet and unassuming but expensive.* The new First Lady's longstanding preference for plain fabrics and what she called 'terribly simple, covered-up clothes' quickly evolved to take in fashionable notch-collar jackets, sleeveless A-line dresses, gloves worn above-the-elbow and low-heeled pumps. Perched atop her trademark bouffant hairdo (styled by Mr Kenneth), Halston's little pillboxes quickly became such an integral part of this look that JFK insisted his wife wear one with a matching bright pink Chanel suit for the couple's open-top drive through Dallas on 22 November 1963.

The sudden, shocking events of that day ensured that both suit and hat were seen by millions, more clearly than they had noticed JFK's top hat at his inauguration only two years

---

* According to *Newsweek*, in 1961 Mrs Kennedy spent $45,446 more on fashion than her husband's $100,000 presidential salary.

earlier. Perhaps for this reason the pillbox** became associated most closely with Jackie Kennedy. It still is, even though in the years following the assassination her appearance changed dramatically as she acquired a taste for billowing trouser suits, silk Hermès headscarves and – especially – large, round, dark sunglasses.

Far more than that of any other First Lady, Jackie's style was copied by mass-marketers and copied with varying degrees of success by large numbers of fashionable young women, both in the US and Europe. London's *Evening Standard* called the effect 'her magic majesty' – even the young Princess of Wales is said to have picked up some tips – and she remained a leading fashion icon years after leaving Washington and becoming Jackie O. For this reason, if, inexplicably, JFK is still to be blamed for the hat's decline – and really he can't be – then his widow's influence on female fashions must surely go a long way to redress the balance.

** This is now lost, although the still-bloodstained pink suit has been preserved by the National Archives in Maryland. It will not go on display until the twenty-second century.

BLACK CAP

If not the most sinister-looking hat in British history (that one surely belonged to a plague doctor, p.37) the judicial black cap must be the most chilling.

Its origins are ancient, which is to say mysterious and likely to remain that way, and really it is much less of a cap than a simple square of black fabric. It is thought to date from Tudor times, which means judges have spent a very long time donning these little black squares immediately prior to sentencing prisoners to death.

So long, that is, that performances of this short, but nevertheless somewhat ghoulish, piece of theatre were still taking place until well into the 1960s. They only ceased after Peter Allen (at Walton Prison in Liverpool) and Gwynne Owen Evans (at Manchester's Strangeways) achieved the joint but unenviable distinction of becoming the last criminals to be hanged in Britain.

The two men were never to know about their achievement, of course, because at the time – 8 o'clock on the morning of 13 August 1964 – theirs were just another pair of entirely routine executions. It was only a couple of months later that the government announced a five-year suspension of the death penalty, which was then finally abolished in 1969. In other words, had the pair waited only a few weeks before bludgeoning a van driver to death so that they could steal £10, both would have lived to tell the tale. A tale which, in this case, included one of them carelessly leaving his overcoat at the scene of the crime, thereby ensuring that both were arrested within a matter of hours …

Since 1964 no British judge has had cause to don the black cap for its grim purpose, but that hasn't stopped members of the judiciary taking the caps into court with them just in case. It's unlikely the tradition is being maintained in the hope that the death penalty will be restored, but rather it is probably being done in much the same way that many of those same judges occasionally carry posies of flowers into morning sessions when these are held at London's Old Bailey.

These small bouquets were meant to provide some protection from the noxious smells and infections emanating from the poor unfortunates left to rot in Newgate Prison next door. Needless to say, this didn't work terribly well. Nor has the fact that the infamous medieval house of horrors was torn down in 1904 been allowed to interfere with a pretty tradition. (It didn't worry crime novelist Margery Allingham either, who, decades later, published another in the best-selling 'Albert Campion' series called *Flowers for the Judge*.)

But of course there's a difference. The flowers are a harmless piece of nostalgia whereas the black cap, strictly speaking, still forms a part of a judge's ceremonial dress, although it's a part most of us have never got to see. Because it's illegal to take photographs when a court is sitting, even images of a black cap *in situ* are vanishingly rare. In fact, possibly the only one is that showing Sir Thomas Townsend Bucknill passing a sentence of death on the Liverpudlian poisoner, Frederick Seddon, back in 1912. (Both Seddon and the judge were freemasons, but any sense of brotherhood was no help at all to the guilty party who was duly hanged at Pentonville).

It's a horribly sobering picture for anyone who knows what he's looking at, and that reason alone makes it even stranger that black caps still exist. For most of us the only way to see one in its right place is to witness the annual ceremony held each November when a new Lord Mayor of London is sworn in for the first time in the Great Hall of the Royal Courts of Justice in the Strand. This is a solemn occasion at which the Lord Chief Justice and two judges of the Queen's Bench Division are present. Each of them is required to appear in full regalia, including this strange square of black cloth, while the Lord Mayor swears that he will 'faithfully perform the duties of my office'.

Worn correctly, the square is draped on top of the judge's horsehair wig, with one corner pointing forward like a widow's peak. From a milliner's point of view there could be no simpler garment but, for all its simplicity, the continuing existence of such a horrible thing is hard to defend.

Most obviously, particularly for anyone who is unhappy with what many see as judicial play-acting – the court's bizarre costumes, the flattery and silly flummery, the expense – it seems extraordinary than an educated man would spend time adjusting his dress before pronouncing a death sentence. Cruel too and more than a little grotesque, when the real point of the proceedings wasn't to give anyone the chance to dress up but to end a person's life.

Judges must still like them, because it's otherwise hard to explain why they continue to carry them around. Certainly Lord Denning was happy to explain to journalists how donning his own black cap to pass a death sentence was something which never troubled him, and he was Master of the Rolls. Mind you, he was also the man who insisted that hanging the Birmingham Six would have saved everyone a lot of fuss, and who didn't feel compelled to amend his opinion even slightly when all six convictions were overturned on appeal.

Admittedly, other judges have been more circumspect. A few have even tried to suggest there's a link with ancient Greek and Roman customs of covering the head as a sign of mourning or respect. But unfortunately there have also always been judges who seemed to display an unhealthy enthusiasm for the things, and even a few who appeared to take a sadistic pleasure in slowly putting one on before announcing the awful inevitability of what was to follow for the hapless prisoner.

Even in its heyday, however, the black cap was never really much of a garment, so surely, more than half a century after Britain's last execution, it is one that we could afford to lose.